a
radical
approach
to
job enrichment

a
radical
approach
to
job enrichment

LYLE YORKS

amacom

A DIVISION OF AMERICAN MANAGEMENT ASSOCIATIONS

658.314
Y 65

160408

658.314

Y 65

160408

Library of Congress Cataloging in Publication Data

Yorks, Lyle.
A radical approach to job enrichment.

Includes index.
1. Job satisfaction. 2. Performance standards.
I. Title.
HF5549.5.J63Y67 658.31'42 75-44481
ISBN 0-8144-5412-7

© 1976 AMACOM
A division of American Management Associations, New York.
All rights reserved. Printed in the United States of America.

This publication may not be reproduced, stored in a retrieval system, or transmitted in whole or in part, in any form or by any means, electronic, mechanical, photocopying, recording, or otherwise, without the prior written permission of AMACOM, 135 West 50th Street, New York, N.Y. 10020.

Second Printing

To Carl H. Thompson, district manager,
Travelers Insurance Companies, whom I was fortunate
to have as my first manager in the business world.
His unselfish approach to his subordinates
was a major influence on my career
and personal development.

preface

This book grows out of my experiences as a consultant working with companies in many diverse industries on employee performance problems. Out of these experiences I have become convinced that many, many times, performance problems are the result not of inadequate employees, but rather of how management has structured the work process.

Time and again I have come in contact with service representatives whose job it is to *not* provide service, of machine operators who have no responsibility for their product and know it, and workers who, when asked to help out, say, "That's not my job," because someone has taken great pains to point out specifically what *is* their job.

It is my belief that these situations evolve not because management is perverse or inattentive or uncaring, but rather as a result of the way in which it traditionally reacts to performance problems. This book suggests that often management's natural reaction intensifies the problems which exist and that alternative, but not so natural, reactions might be more appropriate.

I have written this book for middle and senior managers

and the staff people who serve them. As the reader will soon discover, I argue for a specific point of view: that the way in which we structure work experiences makes a significant difference in how employees perform. I argue this position strongly not because I believe the approach presented here solves all problems—indeed I hope it will become clear that I think any management strategy has associated benefits and costs—but because I believe management seldom considers that approach when confronted with operating problems.

Part One presents a general framework which I believe managers should consider utilizing when trying to understand some of the performance problems with which they find themselves confronted. The remainder of the book discusses alternative ways of structuring work experiences and methods of implementation so that these alternatives work.

The book is incomplete in the sense that I have not tried to present all the alternatives which might logically grow out of the framework offered in Part One—only those which have worked enough times for me to have confidence in their practicality for many work situations. I present those models, experiences, research findings, and management writings which have most influenced my thinking as I have attempted to understand the problems we face in today's organizations.

acknowledgments

Space does not permit mention of all those who have contributed significantly to my thinking and to whom I am therefore grateful.

Among the individuals to whom I feel particularly indebted are the late James D. Thompson, whose teachings and conversation at Vanderbilt provided me with a framework for understanding organizations which still heavily influences my thinking; Mayer Zald, also of Vanderbilt University, whose theories of complex organization behavior and control of institutions have often proved valuable to me in analyzing organizational problems; Norman Edmonds, director of Corporate Management Services and Planning, Travelers Insurance Companies, who early in my career taught me the practical aspects of getting things accomplished in the corporate environment; and John Drake, president of Drake-Beam & Associates, who has provided considerable support in helping me develop my skills as a consultant.

I value my association with all my colleagues at Drake-Beam. Particular mention should be made of James Cabrera, who has given me special encouragement. Robert N. Ford, who is now associated with Drake-Beam, and Bruce Duffany, now with AT&T, have influenced my thinking, and I am thankful for having had the opportunity of being associated with them.

Every now and then we have the opportunity of developing personal relationships with colleagues which truly make a difference in our lives. For me, David Whitsett has been such an individual. Working with and learning from Dave Whitsett has been a singularly unique experience. His influence on the ideas expressed in this book has been so great it would be impossible to give appropriate credit.

Pat Fitzgerald, who suffered through the preparation of several drafts of this manuscript, has my sincere gratitude. Jay Carroll, my editor, has proved particularly valuable in helping me think through the organization of my ideas.

LYLE YORKS

contents

part one

structure, controls, and performance

Organization structure, organization control, and employee performance are interdependent variables. Indeed, the organization's approach to control influences the design of its structure. And an organization's structure has a direct impact upon the behavior and performance of employees.

Chapters 1 and 2 explore the relationships among these three variables. Chapter 3 puts forth some methods of structuring work which build upon the essential nature of these relationships.

1

organization structure and employee performance

How an organization structures the work experiences of its employees has a dominant influence on the performance of those employees. Proper personnel selection and training are important, indeed crucial, concerns for any work organization. But no matter how perfectly the company performs these operations, if the organization is badly structured, performance, in the long run, will be poor.

Employee behavior tends to reflect how management has structured the organization. If employee performance is substandard, the first question management should ask itself is, "What are we doing that causes them to perform poorly?" Frequently it is the organization which needs to change, not the employees. That this is true has been demonstrated to me many times during my consulting career.

For example, several years ago I participated as an instructor in a customer relations course conducted by the Center for Government Training at the University of Tennessee. The client organization was a large public utility whose management was concerned about the quality of work being performed by much of their clerical staff. Productivity was low and quality had been declining over a long period of time. Customer complaints had risen to a point where management was seriously concerned.

Before beginning my formal involvement with the clerical staff, I met with many of them individually and discussed their jobs. I also observed the units at work. The people I came in contact with appeared to be first-rate. Yet the job was not getting done. The reason became clear as the course wore on.

With the clerks' permission, I taped a sampling of phone conversations with customers and discussed conversations of interest with the clerks in the classroom. Each time we pursued a workable alternative to the way a clerk handled a particular situation, we ran up against a rule that prohibited it. Often the clerks would interject, "We used to do it that way, but the system was changed by management." The clerks had little opportunity to arrive at an acceptable solution to a customer's problem; either there was a rule or procedure which got in the way, or a supervisor's approval was required, or the computer system could not handle that type of transaction.

As a result, customers were dissatisfied and the employees' morale suffered because they lacked authority to deal with these encounters on the basis of their experience and knowledge. The company's problem was not with the employees, but with the structure of their jobs.

Unless changes were made in the structure, the employees would not be able to apply any of the skills learned in the course. Indeed, they had not been able to apply skills they already had before attending the course. In this kind of situation, training would not prove effective in improving performance or morale.

My experiences working with various police forces stressed the same point equally well. During the 1960s, emphasis was increasingly placed on behavioral training for police officers as a result of developing tensions in the cities and on campus. The federally funded law-enforcement education program reimbursed police officers' tuition to encourage them to obtain college degrees. Many police academies introduced behavioral science segments in their rookie training curricula. One of the hoped-for outcomes of such training was more positive attitudes among patrolmen toward blacks, students, and other minorities.

As an instructor in many college and police academy courses, I came to doubt that they were having a direct impact on attitudes on the job. In riding with officers on patrol, it became evident that the structure of their work exposed them to pressures and experiences which had far greater influence on their behavior and attitude than schoolwork or training courses. What was intellectually clear to them in the classroom was negated by the realities of the work situation. Even the most idealistic rookie would adopt a negative view of human nature after a year or so of experiencing hostile responses from all segments of society, switching work zones interchangeably with other officers, and being caught in political pressures.

Many young men joined the police force because they thought the work would be interesting and they had a sincere desire to help people, but after a short time on the force they would come to believe that most people could not be trusted. They would soon begin to exhibit very aggressive behavior. Many said they believed their own survival was an issue of constant concern. Very cynical attitudes toward society in general would develop as the young officers met with negative responses from all segments of society. Given the conditions the officers worked under, these attitudes were a predictable development.

Still a third example involves a large metropolitan utility company that was having a hard time keeping experienced operators. The problem was occurring at the point where operations men were to be promoted into control room jobs, the most sophisticated positions in the operations department. Control room operators were responsible for the performance of the total power generating system in the plant. They monitored system performance from a complex console. Should something have begun to go wrong anywhere in the system, these operators were responsible for initiating corrective action.

Large numbers of operators turned down these positions and opted instead for transfer to the maintenance department, a tendency which was costing the utility many of its best operators.

The maintenance department was responsible for repair work and preventive maintenance on the utility's complex equipment and systems. In the area of compensation, the operations and maintenance departments were pegged to each other, with operators and mechanics receiving the same pay at each grade. However, the operator's job was more tedious in that he was confined to a station that always had to be covered, while maintenance crews had physical mobility. Further, if an operator's relief man failed to appear, he was expected to pull an additional shift, whereas a mechanic had a more flexible overtime arrangement. Operators also worked on rotating shifts and pulled more weekend work than maintenance workers.

The company was aware of these problems and mentioned them before the study began. Management felt, however, that in addition to these obvious difficulties, other issues might be involved. Further, the union, while sympathetic to management's problem, was reluctant to permit arbitrary walling-off of the transfer route, because it was so popular with the men.

Interviews on the shop floor revealed other aspects of the organization that were associated with the problem of operator transfers. For example, although it appeared that a certain type of temperament might be better suited to control room work, no selection and placement activity was carried out along these lines. Interviews with foremen revealed that men were usually hired for whatever department they requested on the basis of available job openings. This was verified by the personnel department.

The interviews also indicated that training was haphazard on all levels. Operators reported that they just followed the more experienced operators around and did what they were told. Usually it was a direct command like "Turn that wheel" or "Push that button." Explanations were not often forthcoming. The result was that at lower levels of the operations department hierarchy, there was little comprehension of the total system. Statements such as these were common: "You really don't know what you're doing," "After a while you begin to know when to do something, but you're never sure why," and "It's really interesting how the system works, but to learn about it, you're on your own."

This situation existed despite the fact the company had set up elaborate simulation control rooms which could be used for both selection and training purposes. However, men were not exposed to the simulators until they already were in control room jobs. Thus, improved selection and training activities were obvious elements of any strategy for solving the operator transfer problem.

Further investigation revealed additional aspects of the problem which were structural in nature. Advanced operators (but not yet advanced enough for control room positions) were assigned as spare hands to maintenance crews. They functioned much like apprentices, helping with tools, running errands, assisting in repair work, and so forth. Typical attitudinal responses from men in these positions were, "Returning to a full-time operating job would be a step back, after working my way up here" or "The maintenance guys get to see the results of their work. In operations, I never did." During their tenure with the maintenance crews, operators were gradually being socialized into the maintenance job. They began to identify strongly with their new department, accepting the attitudes and expectations of the regular crew members.

Further, many operators saw the control room as overwhelming: "When something goes wrong, they jump all over those guys." "The way I see it, if you give a man a job, you should believe he knows what he's doing." "First sign of trouble and all the brass is in there second-guessing him." One operator in a lower-level job classification commented, "Once one of the generators started to go. They lined us all up in there so we would be available. Man, management took over the control room. I didn't know what was happening, but I decided I didn't want any part of that place."

Talking with the control room operators revealed that most liked their jobs and saw them as challenging: "They had to talk me into coming in here. For three weeks I was scared to death, but once you learn what it's all about, it's OK." "If some of these guys would try it, they would find out it isn't as bad as it looks." "I never understood how the plant worked before I came in here. I was scared at first, but they kind of pushed me into it. Now I'm glad they did."

Direct observation indicated the control room jobs were fairly enriched. The operators had a clear work module with plenty of responsibility. Feedback was immediate. The only obvious problems were that under normal conditions the job was pretty routine (although interviews indicated acceptance of this fact), and that in time of crisis management artificially introduced too much pressure.

It was clear that in addition to implementing changes in selection and training procedures, management had to change the structure of the lower-level operations jobs so that operators experienced more positively what was involved in control room work. Failure to do so would limit the effect of any improvement in selection and training of new men.

The specific nature of structural solutions to these types of problems is the content of later chapters. For now, these cases are meant to illustrate the influence organization structure has on employee behavior. These, and many similar experiences, have convinced me that personnel selection and training can succeed only if work experiences are properly structured by management.

Therefore, a principal objective of managers should be effective management of work structure. Effective management of work structure means utilizing human resources to the fullest extent so that employees are able to contribute as much as they want to the satisfaction of the firm's objectives. How managers manage the work structure of their organization affects employee behavior and attitudes either negatively or positively in a significant way and ultimately affects organization performance in the same manner.

ORGANIZATION STRUCTURE DEFINED

If organization structure is to be a major variable in the management of human resources, then it should be more explicitly defined. Generally, structure refers to *any empirical system consisting of relationships between elements of the system.*[1] That is to say, an observable set of points (either individuals, work stations, girders of a building, and so on) relate to each other to form a system. Organizations are composed of several systems, such as formal reporting relationships, technical production flows, informal power relationships, information systems, and the like. Each organization system has been referred to at one time or another in the literature on management and organization as an aspect of organization structure. Organization structure is best viewed as a composite concept—the combination and interrelationships of several structural systems.

For our purposes, organization structure refers to those aspects of the organization which form observable patterns of work relationships. Superior-subordinate reporting relationships, work flow patterns and the resultant employee interfaces, job content (activities an individual performs in carrying out his job), and interdepartmental relationships and information flows are all dimensions of an organization's structure. Each represents a definable empirical system within the organization, each can be charted or diagramed, and each combines with the others to create the general framework through which the organization performs.

We can further clarify this definition by applying it to the three organizational examples discussed earlier. At the public utility the procedures and regulations which set the limits of employee action, the extent to which employees were able to perform their jobs without seeking supervisory approval, and the limitations of the data processing system all reflect organization structure. Similarly, in the second example the method of assignment of police officers, conditions of contact with the public, and political interference from superiors all reflect structural realities confronting the police officer. The same is true of the operators of the metropolitan utility with regard to the manner in which they interfaced with control room operators as compared with maintenance crews. This will become clearer as we continue.

THE NATURE OF ORGANIZATION STRUCTURE

Organizations are both *intangible* and, compared with physical structures, more *variable* in nature. Organizations are intangible because they are primarily social entities. As such, their structures are systems of events (activities, happenings, behaviors) rather than systems of physical parts.[2]

This distinction between physical and social entities is important. Physical structures can be identified even when they are not functioning. The structure of a building is visible even if the building is deserted, and an airplane still exists even when it is not in use.

When a social system, such as an organization, stops functioning, its structure dissolves and no longer exists. As Daniel Katz and Robert Kahn have observed, social structures have no anatomy or physiology which exists apart from the functioning of the organization itself.[3] The structure of an organization consists of the processes in which it is engaged. This element of intangibility tends to make thinking in terms of organization structure difficult for those working within the organization.

Their intangible nature makes organizations highly variable as well. The structure of an organization is variable because it is held together not by any set of physical or biological givens but by the psychological anchorings of the attitudes, perceptions, beliefs, habits, and expectations of its members.[4] The following factors introduce into the structure of the organization elements of variability which can affect employee performance and need to be controlled by the manager:

1. An individual's attitudes, expectations, and beliefs are not constants but vary over time.

2. Most organizations recruit members from a broad spectrum of society, thereby introducing several different psychological sets into the structure.

3. The organization cannot demand total commitment from the individuals it employs. Rather, it must share the human elements which are the determinant points for most of its structure with competing interests such as family, community, recreation, and other personal pursuits.

THE EFFECTS OF ORGANIZATION STRUCTURE ON MANAGEMENT BEHAVIOR

The essential nature of organization structure affects managerial behavior in two important ways:

1. Its *intangible* nature leads to a tendency of management to overlook the influence of structure on employee behavior.

2. Because organization structure is so highly *variable*, control becomes an essential concern of management.

Let us consider each of these two issues in more detail.

The Influence of Structure Is Overlooked

Managers have long recognized the impact of organization structure on organizational performance at the macro level (for example, witness the widespread recognition of the contributions of Alfred Sloan at General Motors and the always prevalent discussions of corporate structure in business magazines).

However, managers have tended to ignore the impact structure has on performance at the micro level (individual performance), partly because in their minds organization structure, as it relates to employees, is a dependent variable. That is to say, the situation which confronts the individual as he fills his role in the organization is seen by managers as a given.

Existing structure is seen to be the result of a series of conditions, such as technology, labor agreements, competitive business conditions, mass production, mass labor, and so forth. There is little that can be done about it. Further, management is likely to view the present structure as necessary if the firm is to have predictability in its internal affairs.

For example, many managers argue that variability of employee behavior results in controls which reinforce more rigid organization structure. Thus, the structure of the situation in which employees must perform their duties is seen as a result of the need for control in the organization. The need for control is the result of the behavior of employees themselves.

Also contributing to the tendency of managers to overlook the impact of structure on employee behavior is the fact that managers themselves are part of the structure. At the macro level, structural analysis involves viewing the organization as an open system interacting with its environment. Management is in effect stepping outside the organization and approaching it as an entity in and of itself. At the micro level, however, where the issues involve how organization structure is affecting employee behavior, it is difficult for the manager to make a detached analysis because his behavior constitutes a significant element in the structure.

Finally, because an organization structure is composed of so many different elements, many of which are just "the way things are," it is difficult for managers to conceptualize its effects on behavior and performance. Because it is intangible, organization structure is ignored, and many managers are simply unaware of it as a reality.

The tendency of managers to view organization structure as a given, coupled with their difficulty in perceiving the impact of their own behavior patterns as part of that structure, results in the adoption of "change the person" strategies for dealing with employee problems. Counseling and resocializing employees through pep talks, company literature or workshops, more training, and in extreme instances, transfer or termination are the most typical approaches to employee performance problems. What all these activities share in common is the objective of producing an employee who better fits his job.

In many situations, application of these techniques is appropriate and effective in dealing with the problem. In a good many other instances it is not. Performance remains unsatisfactory. The manager becomes puzzled and attributes the problem to the general poor quality of the work force available to him.

Controls as an Essential Concern of Management

An alternative to "change the people" strategies is the implementation of controls in the form of increased monitoring of performance through reports, work rules, and procedures, and increased involvement of superiors in the work functions of the employees. If management cannot change employee behavior, it can at least police it. Unhappily, such controls apply not only to the offending employees but are usually implemented on all employees.

Controls are efforts at reducing the degree of variability in an organization. As such, they are meant to reinforce an organization's structure. However, they become part of the structure they reinforce. Implementation of new controls is a structural change on the part of the organization. This point becomes clearer when we examine more closely the typical kinds of controls instituted in such situations:

1. Direct supervisory controls in the form of increasing the number of supervisors, requiring them to check or approve certain production activities, generally requiring them to issue more direct commands and report to management more frequently, or some other direct behavioral change on their part.

Such changes directly affect the content of the jobs of both supervisors and subordinates, and the manner in which these people relate to each other. The manner, frequency, and reasons for interfacing between supervisors and subordinates is altered, effecting an observable structural change.

2. Statistical indexes which measure and summarize specific aspects of employee behavior. This information is compared against a performance standard by management. Any deviation from acceptable standards requires explanation on the part of

supervision and lower level managers and usually results in additional direct supervisory controls.

Compiling data for these reports becomes a regular activity of supervision and employees. Thus, both information flows and job content are directly affected. In extreme situations, managing the flow of reports becomes a major objective of first-line supervisors and lower level management.

3. Formal procedures which are written up and distributed. Any situation which requires deviation from the procedures most often requires approval from a manager. Once again, job content is directly affected. The range of discretion of job incumbents is limited, and the interface between worker and superior is once again affected.

All three of the controls discussed share a common element: They represent a strengthening of the locus of control in a part of the organization other than the target population. An attempt is made at imposing control on a group of individuals from outside the group itself. As such, we will refer to them as *organizational controls.*

STRUCTURAL CHANGE AS A BEHAVIOR CHANGE STRATEGY

An increasing body of evidence suggests that structure changes in organizations force behavior changes resulting in significant changes in employee attitudes and expectations. Wallace Wohlking has reviewed an extensive body of literature which supports the structural change–behavior change–attitude change model as an influential dynamic affecting behavior in organizations.[5]

Wohlking's article reviews several examples of structural changes which resulted in positive behavior and attitude changes. Among them are Robert Ford's experiments in job enrichment at AT&T,[6] Eric Trist's work with British coal miners through changing the composition of work teams,[7] and measured changes in the attitudes of white department store workers toward black employees following equal-status contact situations resulting from the enactment of a New York State employment antidiscrimination law.[8]

In each of these instances changes which required employees to behave differently on the job resulted in attitudinal changes. Several examples not cited by Wohlking support the same model of behavior change, including Texas Instruments' work with cleaning personnel [9] and studies of attitudes of blacks and whites toward living in the same residential buildings in public housing.[10] In general, the model suggested by these experiences is that structural changes in the social situation of an individual which force perceivable changes in his behavior patterns will result in attitudinal changes on his part.

The dynamics of this model are suggestive of weaknesses in some change-the-person strategies. For example, training is often prescribed in the belief that it will lead to an attitude change which will lead to a behavior change back on the job. This strategy often does not work because the employee leaves the training situation to confront a work structure which does not allow for utilization of the new skills or ideas obtained through the training. The result is that the employee either reverts to the original behavior and attitudes or experiences extreme frustration.

This is the sequence of events which occurred in both the Tennessee utility and police force training situations described at the beginning of this chapter. Without accompanying changes in the structured work experiences of the employees involved, the desired attitude changes did not transfer into behavior changes back on the job.

However, structural change can produce not only positive changes in behavior and attitude, but negative as well. For example, Wohlking cites the classic study by Warner and Low in which the introduction of mass production methods set off a chain of events which led to intense labor-management conflict.[11] Returning to our discussion of controls, it will be recalled that implementing *organization* controls involved structural change. Such controls do affect employee behavior. As management intended, they restrict employee behavior. Supervision is more involved in the day-to-day, hour-to-hour, and even minute-to-minute aspects of production. These controls often elicit unanticipated dysfunctional effects on behavior and attitudes.

Gene Dalton and Paul Lawrence of the Harvard Business School have identified two types of dysfunctional effects of these kinds of controls: those which grow out of compliance and those which grow out of resistance.[12]

In dysfunctional impacts growing out of compliance, the controls become an end in themselves. Procedures are followed even when they are clearly inappropriate. Or departments attempt to remain in budget, or to hit a production standard even in the face of changing conditions which may make the standard unrealistic and will result in disagreeable consequences in the future. The organization becomes rigid and unresponsive and no longer adapts easily to unanticipated demands by its environment. Employees become procedure-oriented and hesitant to perform any tasks not specifically required of them.

The second response pattern involves a rebellion of employees who find controls interfering with their ability to perform their job. Sometimes resistance is subtle, emerging as apathy or lack of trying. Other times it becomes more overt, with the employee trying to beat the system. Either response is likely to be advanced by managers as examples of employee problems which necessitate the controls. Thus, managers fail to understand the essential nature of the impact of structural change as a causal variable operating on behavior. They fail to recognize that it is the controls which may be precipitating the "problem" behavior.

Many executives acknowledge that each of these two response patterns occurs regularly in business organizations. And each can become a major problem affecting the performance of the organization. Given our current knowledge of the effect of structural change on behavior and attitudes, such responses are understandable and, to an extent, predictable.

Alvin Gouldner in his classic, *Patterns of Industrial Bu-*

reaucracy, has provided a detailed set of illustrations regarding the dysfunctional impact of organizational controls as a response to employee performance problems. For example:

> If a supervisor viewed a worker as unmotivated, as unwilling to "do a job," how did the supervisor respond? How did he attempt to solve this problem? He usually attempted to handle this by directing the worker more closely, by watching him carefully, and explicitly outlining his work obligations. As one foreman said, "If I catch a man goofing off, I tell him in an ABC way, exactly what he has to do and I watch him like a hawk till he has done it."

> At first glance this might appear tc be a stable solution; it might seem as if "close supervision" would allow the supervisor to bring the problem under control. Actually, however, there were commanding reasons why supervisors could not rest content to supervise their workers closely and to remind them endlessly of what had to be done. One motive was fairly obvious: the supervisor could not watch all of his men all of the time. As a surface foreman remarked, "As soon as I turn my back on some of these guys, they slip me the knife."

> There is, however, another consideration that made close supervision a dangerous solution to the problem of the unmotivated worker. Specifically, workers view close supervision as a kind of "strictness" and punishment. In consequence, the more a supervisor watched his subordinates, the more hostile they became to him.[13]

At another point, Gouldner notes:

> Just as the rules facilitated punishment, so too did they define the behavior which could permit punishment to be escaped. The rule served as a specification of a *minimum* level of acceptable performance. It was therefore possible for the worker to remain apathetic, for he now knew just how *little* he could do and still remain secure.[14]

Gouldner's observations illustrate well the dysfunctional influence which organizational controls such as direct supervision and bureaucratic procedures can have on employee behavior.

His research emphasizes how structural changes such as these precipitate negative employee behavior.

In my own consulting career I have experienced similar situations. Working with a closely supervised clerical operation where, as part of a job enrichment effort, supervision allowed selected employees to exercise more decision making over their jobs, a supervisor was approached by a clerk who asked to be placed on the new "program."

This particular employee had been written up twice (a procedure for documenting formal reprimands concerning performance; three documented instances meant a clerk could be terminated). Because of her absenteeism, she was the last clerk the supervisor was prepared to let have more autonomy. On the other hand, she was very intelligent and resented the close supervision, feeling she was treated like a child.

When the supervisor asked what she should do, I suggested she discuss with the clerk what standards had to be maintained if the clerk was to have her job changed. She sat down with the clerk and agreed to implement job changes, while the clerk agreed to meet attendance standards. The clerk responded to the changed situation and nine months later was no longer under documentation.

The public utility in Tennessee discussed earlier also comes to mind. Again, management had instituted strict organization controls, mainly in the form of procedures and direct supervision, and usually under the framework of "standardization which gives us better control."

Unfortunately, the standardization gave management little control over the performance of their organization. They had fallen victim to the widely held myth that rigid standardization yields control, and that belief was producing a false sense of security.

Management had successfully minimized the range of discretion of the clerks, and the result was poor customer service due to the way accounts were handled. Supervisors who had authority to take action were both overworked and one level removed from the actual work flow process. Thus, despite standardization, they were not in a position to make informed decisions.

Many of the experienced customer services clerks resented the restrictions. Others had become apathetic toward their jobs. Through it all, management was insensitive to the kind of performance many of their employees were capable of giving the organization were procedures changed to allow them to do so.

Structural changes in the form of job content, patterns of interaction required by work flow, supervisory behavior, and procedures can be expected to influence employee behavior. The nature of the change determines whether the influence will be primarily of a positive or negative nature. The problem then is identification of a common denominator which can provide management with a reference point for predicting whether a structural change will influence behavior positively or negatively. The search for this common denominator begins with an examination of the relationship between controls and employee motivation. This is the topic of Chapter 2.

REFERENCES

1. Frank Harary, Robert Z. Norman, and Dorwin Cartwright, *Structural Models: An Introduction to the Theory of Directed Graphs* (New York: John Wiley & Sons, 1965).

2. Daniel Katz and Robert L. Kahn, *The Social Psychology of Organizations* (New York: John Wiley & Sons, 1966), p. 31.

3. Ibid.

4. Ibid., p. 33.

5. Wallace Wohlking, "Attitude Change, Behavior Change: The Role of the Training Department," *California Management Review*, vol. 13, no. 2 (winter 1970).

6. Robert N. Ford, *Motivation through the Work Itself* (New York: American Management Associations, 1969).

7. Eric Trist et al., *Organization Choice* (London: Tavistock Institute of Human Relations, 1962).

8. John Harding and Russell Hogrefe, "Attitudes of White Department Store Employees toward Negro Co-workers," *Journal of Social Issues,* vol. 8, no. 1 (1952).

9. Harold M. Rush, *Job Design for Motivation* (New York: The Conference Board, 1971).

10. Morton Deutsch and Mary Evans Collins, "Interracial Housing," in William Petersen, ed., *American Social Patterns* (New York: Doubleday Anchor Books, 1956).

11. Lloyd Warner and J. O. Low, *The Social System of the Modern Factory,* Yankee City Series, vol. 4 (New Haven: Yale University Press, 1947).

12. Gene W. Dalton and Paul R. Lawrence, *Motivation and Control in Organizations* (Homewood, Ill.: Dorsey Press, 1971), p. 8.

13. Alvin W. Gouldner, *Patterns of Industrial Bureaucracy* (New York: The Free Press, 1954), p. 159. Reprinted with permission of Macmillan Publishing Co., Inc. Copyright 1954 by The Free Press.

14. Ibid., p. 174. Reprinted with permission, as stated.

2

controls and the motivation
of employee behavior

Control and motivation are interrelated issues. The activity of control refers in great part to the ability of management to regulate employee behavior.[1] If, to the manager, control involves regulation of behavior, its success requires compliance on the part of employees.

The employee may comply from a desire to obtain some good or privilege from management; from his sense of obligation either to his dependents, to the company, to co-workers, or to the job itself; from his personal interest and involvement in the job; or from some similar personal desire to respond. In short, management's success in regulating employee behavior depends on employee motivation—"motivation" being defined as those forces within an individual that push or propel him to satisfy basic needs or wants.

All control systems make assumptions about worker motivation to comply. Incentive and piecework systems assume employee financial needs are strong enough to insure employee compliance with production standards. Increased direct supervision assumes a lack of motivation toward work short of holding on to the job. The team approach to production, which is currently being experimented with in some companies, relies heavily on assumptions about employee motivation to not let down peers and willingness to respond to peer group pressure, as well as employee needs for more freedom on the job.

Those are elements of control strategies which are currently being utilized, either independently or in combination with other elements, by American industry for the regulation of employee behavior. Each rests on certain assumptions about worker motivation for compliance.

Although these assumptions are seldom articulated by managers, they are present nonetheless. For example, when the possibilities of various control systems are pursued with managers in a consulting situation, they will often exclaim, "But, you understand, I have to keep my eyes on these guys every minute," or "I don't think most of them would leave their buddies in the lurch," or some other comment indicative of basic assumptions regarding employee motivation to work.

Such views set the limits to what kinds of changes managers will agree to and influence greatly the character of existing control systems within the company. Whether or not managers feel comfortable in discussing "assumptions about human nature," they all hold such assumptions and these set the parameters of their behavior as managers.

In this chapter, we will consider more closely the relationship between worker motivation and different approaches to control. The emphasis will be on the forces which produce compliance. We will begin with a discussion of worker motivation.

MOTIVATION AND WORK

A comment often heard from managers in all walks of business life is, "My main problem is finding motivated people." A corollary to that is the remark that "The biggest part of my job is motivating my people. The mark of a good leader is the ability to inspire a high level of performance from subordinates."

Such attitudes are significant because they reflect a series of underlying assumptions which greatly influence the strategies adopted by managers in trying to solve "people problems," assumptions which a mounting body of evidence indicates are erroneous in what they emphasize about human behavior.

Specifically, the assumptions in question are (1) motivation leads to achievement and (2) motivation is a force which exists external to an individual. These two are not, in and of themselves, part of any tightly reasoned system of logic regarding motivation. I mention them together because, in one form or another, they repeatedly turn up in discussions with managers. Their influence is felt in the conclusions to which they typically lead supervisors regarding strategies for attempting to improve employee performance. In one form or another, these strategies for improving performance reflect a third crucial assumption: (3) changing an employee's attitude will lead to changed behavior on the job.

The strategies for improving employee performance which these assumptions lead managers to implement involve somehow changing people's attitudes, or "plugging in" motivation, so that they will go out and achieve. These assumptions, then, underlie the "change the person" strategy discussed in Chapter 1. *refs to p'3.*

Managers who make these assumptions utilize regular pep talks aimed at getting the employee to identify with the goals of the firm, perhaps emphasizing the crucial role his or her job plays in American society. Or additional training is prescribed for employees. Or periodic contests between workers are held. All of these techniques are efforts at plugging in motivation through attitude change.

Chapter 1 suggested the utility of reversing assumption 3 by exploring the possibility that changing employee behavior first will lead to changed attitudes on the job. The key to changing behavior, it was suggested, lies in the structure of the work situation.

The basis for this alternative model is found in reversing the order of causality in assumptions 1 and 2. In other words, assume that (1) achievement leads to motivation and (2) motivation is a force internal to an individual. These two assumptions underlie the structural change model presented in Chapter 1.

In this view, motivation is seen as a personal experience between an individual and a given situation. Success, or a positive experience, with a given task creates a willingness to do the task again. Thus, in considering structural change, if the change is a positive one, that is, one which provides the opportunity to achieve, the result is increased motivation on the job. On the other hand, if the change is a negative one (one which frustrates the need to achieve or results in feelings of failure), the result will be decreased motivation on the job.

Douglas McGregor was one of the first writers to suggest that a manager does not motivate anyone, but rather that motivation is built into us.[2] It was McGregor's view that we all have unsatiated needs which we are trying to fulfill and which drive us to behave in a certain way. Managers cannot plug in motivation; they only can create conditions where employees find the opportunity to meet these needs.

This understanding of motivation suggests that when a general manager of a large manufacturing plant watched workers run to their cars at the end of shift and said, "Why can't we motivate our men?" he was asking the wrong question. His workers were certainly motivated. Anyone running as fast as they were is certainly motivated.

A better question would have been, "What is motivating our men to leave the plant in such a hurry?" The point is that all behavior requires motivation. A totally unmotivated person would be docile, completely unresponsive, and probably hospitalized in a psychiatric ward. For management the issue is one of channeling motivation, not creating it.

The motivation to work is an internal force. It cannot be plugged in; it is already there. A manager can only try to tap it. Structural changes will influence this internal drive in either a positive or negative fashion. To summarize our argument at a higher level of generality, structural changes which pro-

vide opportunities for employees to satisfy important needs
will generate a motivated work force. Structural changes which
do not allow for need satisfaction will result in less motivated
behavior on the job.

ACHIEVEMENT AS A SPECIFIC NEED

Achievement is a specific need which appears to have a powerful effect on people. In reviewing research on the relationship between achievement and the motivation to work, Michael
Argyle states, "The most common result is that success leads
to greater efforts, failure to less. However, among those who
fail or are told they have failed, the greatest effort is made by
those closest to the target." [3]

Properly used, feedback can provide opportunities for
achievement on the job. Laboratory research, as well as live
industrial experiences, indicates that knowledge of results increases work motivation. For this reason, the feedback dimension of job design has a powerful effect upon work behavior.
Proper management of the feedback dimension can make work
more satisfying, by providing an opportunity to see the results
of one's efforts, and can reinforce teamwork. Improper management of feedback can result in apathy and employees working
at cross-purposes.

For example, a large real estate firm had a group of top
salesmen who continued to improve in performance, and a
considerable number of mediocre performers. Like many real
estate offices, this one encouraged competition among sales
associates through quarterly contests, continuous posting of
sales volume, and similar devices. While such activities are
known to be effective in influencing top performers, their impact is minimal on the average salesmen who feel they have
little chance in competition with the "stars."

In this instance, the same men won all the awards every
year. No matter how much the others improved, the top producers still did better. Good job design dictates that competition with oneself is as important as, if not more important than,

competition with others because in competition with oneself, everyone can improve his position. Altering the performance indexes so that self-improvement was emphasized, as well as total performance, had a positive effect on many of the mediocre performers.

Research has long revealed that work measurement systems which emphasize only one aspect of the job, such as individual productivity, can have a detrimental effect on teamwork. This is particularly harmful on work situations where interpersonal cooperation is essential. Feedback which emphasizes team effort is crucial here. In short, people seem to have an intrinsic need to keep score with themselves, and respond to whatever criteria are available to them for doing so. This seems closely related to the positive effects of feelings of achievement as a motivator.

OTHER NEEDS

Psychologists have identified needs other than achievement which appear to affect behavior. One of these needs is affiliation, a basic desire for social interaction with other people. Research indicates that this need appears to be particularly strong when people are under duress, such as when they are anxious, or confused, or unsure of their self-worth. It is under these conditions that individuals are particularly likely to seek support from their associates.

Industry has discovered that jobs which do not allow for social contact have higher absenteeism and turnover rates than those that do. Thus, ignoring affiliation needs can be costly.

Some companies have attempted to utilize the need for affiliation for increased production and quality on the job. This is one aspect of team approaches to production. In addition to providing more variety and personal control in the work situation, team production aims at creating a cohesive work group. There is some evidence that, in jobs involving social interaction, cohesive groups work harder than uncohesive ones.[4] Further, in cohesive groups, peer group pressure operates as an effective leverage point in directing behavior.

Job enrichment need equity

J. Stacy Adams has advanced a theory that people have a need for *equity*.[5] He suggests that workers try to maintain equity between their inputs (abilities, efforts, experience, etc.) and rewards (pay, benefits, status, other rewards), and are motivated to reduce any inequity. For example, studies show hourly paid workers work harder if they perceive they are overpaid and less hard if they perceive they are underpaid. Under a piecework compensation system, overpaid workers have reduced production and improved quality.[6]

Research has confirmed many of the predictions of equity theory under experimental conditions, and the data are convincing enough to include equity as a potentially motivating force.

Perhaps the most general of the need theories, and the most widely known to businessmen, is the need hierarchy of Abraham Maslow.[7] Maslow identifies five basic levels of needs:

1. Physiological needs (the need for food, water, air, rest, and so on).
2. Safety needs (the need for security).
3. Belongingness needs (the need for social acceptance).
4. Esteem needs (needs for feeling of achievement and recognition or respect from others).
5. Self-actualization needs (needs for feeling the realization of one's potential).

Maslow's theory states that the five needs are ranked in order of importance, with the lowest level, or physiological, needs being the most important. Behavior is motivated by the need which is unsatisfied at the moment. Because lower level needs are more basic, they must be satisfied before higher level needs become operative as motivators.

Maslow does suggest that the exact ordering of the hierarchy is not rigid and may vary in some people. However, physiological needs are seen as always being the lowest level and most important needs, and self-actualization the highest level and least important needs.

While the Maslow need hierarchy makes intuitive sense

to enrich a job you must satisfy need

and seems to explain much about human behavior in the work situation, it is difficult to test empirically. Therefore, solid empirical evidence does not exist. Further, Maslow's categories are very general and, beyond providing managers with a broad framework for understanding motivation and behavior, do not contribute much toward suggesting specific strategies for dealing with motivational problems.

However, Maslow's work has made a major contribution in focusing managers' attention on the intrinsic forces which affect behavior. It has been a central statement directing research into the wants and needs of individuals as a basic cause of behavior.

THE JOB AND MOTIVATION

Since the late 1950s the nature of the job a worker is assigned to do has received widespread recognition as an important factor affecting worker motivation. The research of Frederick Herzberg has been a central force in this focus on the nature of the job itself. Herzberg contends that work which is designed to allow employees to satisfy needs for achievement, recognition, responsibility, advancement, and growth is the basis for employee motivation on the job.

In 1959, Herzberg and two colleagues, Bernard Mausner and Barbara Bloch Snyderman, published research results which indicated that the intrinsic nature of the job has more impact on worker motivation than any other factor.[8] Further, Herzberg argued that the total work situation can be dichotomized:

One of the two parts of the work situation is made up of factors external to the job, such as pay, status, supervisory style, interpersonal relationships, working conditions, company policy, and the like. These factors are environmental to the job itself. They have to do with how a worker is *treated*.

The other part of the work situation is the job itself and whether it affords opportunity for the worker to experience achievement, recognition, responsibility, advancement, and growth. These factors have to do with how a worker is *utilized*.

Herzberg maintained that environmental factors are important, but they operate in a manner different from the impact of the job itself. If the environmental factors are not maintained at the level of worker expectations, that is to say, if workers perceive themselves to be treated unfairly, they will be dissatisfied. And this dissatisfaction will translate into negative behavior on the job (absenteeism, turnover, work restriction, and the like).

However, meeting worker expectations in this area will not particularly result in a highly motivated work force. Rather, it will only serve to limit dissatisfaction. In other words, when the environmental factors operate on work or behavior, they operate in a negative sense. Keeping up with worker expectations regarding how they are treated, Herzberg suggested, is a constant challenge for management because such expectations are constantly rising.

True motivation, according to Herzberg, can be obtained only through the work itself. He views motivation as a direct personal experience between the worker and his job. While working conditions, high pay, and fair supervision may attract a good work force to a company, only challenging utilization of people can motivate them on the job itself.

Herzberg's contribution to managerial thinking is unquestionable in at least two ways. First, the Herzberg model has focused managers' attention on the importance of work itself as a factor influencing motivation and has done so in an easily understandable fashion with at least high intuitive validity for managers. Second, it has made managers realize that they cannot achieve good results by buying off a lack of motivators in the job itself with environmental factors.

Herzberg collected his data using the critical incident method: Workers were asked to discuss a time in their work history which was particularly dissatisfying and then a period which was particularly satisfying.

Herzberg's research has been duplicated, with similar results, on workers from several socioeconomic categories and nationalities. However, researchers using different research techniques have not achieved the same pattern of results. This discrepancy has suggested that the methodology of the research influenced the results and has fueled a debate among industrial psychologists on the extent to which Herzberg's formal theory should be accepted.

In spite of the debate among the theorists, the idea that job design influences worker motivation and performance is widely accepted and has a broad base of data to support it. L. L. Cummings and A. M. El Salmi, for example, maintain that either set of factors, environmental or the work itself, affects both dissatisfaction and motivation.[9] Thus, they argue with Herzberg's theory per se and not with the suggestion that job design influences motivation.

Edward Lawler and Richard Hackman have presented impressive data showing a relationship between job design characteristics and work satisfaction, motivation, and performance.[10] Lawler has widely researched the issue of motivation in organizations, especially the importance of pay as a factor in motivation, and has concluded that there is considerable research evidence that job design influences motivation, job performance, and job satisfaction.

Arthur Turner and Paul Lawrence of the Harvard Business School have published results similar to those of Lawler and Hackman, although their data have also raised the question of how cultural and sociological experiences affect an individual's response to job characteristics.[11]

Thus, there *is* research evidence that job design has a significant positive or negative impact upon employee motivation, depending on whether or not the job allows for the satisfaction of important employee needs. The principal disagreement among many researchers is not on whether the job itself is a crucial factor affecting motivation to work but rather on the degree to which this factor makes a difference in performance relative to other factors such as pay, security, and working conditions and social background. As will be seen later in this book, these theoretical questions have counterparts in the world of practical experience.

To summarize, motivation involves the satisfaction of personal needs. Job structure has a direct effect on need satisfaction. How jobs are structured affects opportunities for experiencing achievement, gaining recognition, advancing and developing oneself, and establishing relationships with co-workers. All those factors contribute to motivation in the workplace.

CONTROL AS ACTION

Now that the dynamics of motivation have been considered, a similar examination into the nature of control will prove useful. The crucial element in control is the location of the right to decide to adjust some aspect of the work situation: stop a machine, work overtime, initiate maintenance, rewrite a letter, make an exception, hire or fire, purchase material, and so forth.

Statistics, budgets, procedures, reviewers, and checkers are not controls. They are vehicles of control. Control exists only when some individual reacts to the information provided by any of these vehicles in order to make an adjustment. Wherever the right to make a particular adjustment is lodged, management is making a commitment that that individual is motivated to exercise control for the benefit of the organization.

Of course, exercising effective control requires more than proper motivation. Two other elements are necessary: adequate information regarding the kind of situation which can be weighed against known organization objectives, and knowledge of cause and effect relationships which are influencing the situation. More simply, the person exercising control needs to know what the situation is and to have an understanding of how to change it. The elements of effective control can be summarized as follows:

Effective control = motivation + appropriate and timely
information + technical knowledge

Control, then, is an action taken for purposes of adjustment. Its effectiveness depends upon the motivation of the individual taking the action, the basis on which he is acting, and his understanding of the effects of his action.

Previously, we referred to certain approaches to control as organization controls. These controls involved direction from elements of the organization other than the target population. The essential characteristic which they all shared was that the receiving of relevant information and the right to initiate adjustments was primarily lodged in these other elements.

The receiving of relevant information and the right to make adjustments in the production process can be lodged within the target group itself, with either the employee or, in some situations, a work crew or team performing a specific job.

Controls that involve direction from the employee can be called *personal controls,* and those that derive from a crew or team can be termed *group controls.* Both assume that if given the proper information and training, employees will act in a responsible manner toward their jobs.

Experience from several industries increasingly suggests that under certain conditions, personal controls and group controls are more effective than organization controls in maintaining good performance. Indeed, implementing group or personal controls is a structural change which can result in positive behavior and attitude changes in employees.

Cryovac, a division of W. R. Grace, found it possible to realize considerable savings in labor costs through job redesign in their manufacturing plants which produce plastic bag wrap.[12] Among the changes made were giving machine operators the authority to stop machines to make quality adjustments, the right to initiate maintenance on machines, and the right to schedule production jobs which had to be run off over the course of a week.

Implementing those changes required that operators receive lab reports and other information on product quality on a regular basis and be given production deadline schedules. Both sources of information were previously received only by the foreman. These changes represented a commitment to personal controls.

Richard Walton has reported on the General Foods pet food plant in Topeka, Kansas, which is operated by work crews of 7 to 14 employees.[13] The crews are given the information on plant performance and managerial decision rules and guidelines. Among the decision-making and control functions performed by each crew are task assignments, dealing with production problems, redistributing task assignments to cover for absent co-workers, and counseling those crew members who do not meet minimum performance standards.

Results have been most impressive, especially with regard to labor costs. The Topeka plant is operated with considerable emphasis on group controls.

FEEDBACK FOR PERSONAL CONTROL
AS POSITIVE STRUCTURAL CHANGE

Through structuring work so that workers can exercise personal control, many of the dysfunctional outcomes of direct organization controls by superiors can be avoided. Feedback, in the form of information flows, is one dimension of work structure which can effectively provide the opportunity for personal control.

In most of the companies I have consulted with, the feedback process relative to specific jobs operates as follows: A worker does the job. Information on how well the job was performed, either in the form of reports or customer reaction, is conveyed to the supervisor, who, if the employee is to receive any feedback, must close the loop. (See Exhibit 1.)

If the job goes smoothly, the supervisor (if he is up on his human relations) periodically informs the worker he is performing well. If something goes amiss, the supervisor has to go to the worker to find out what happened. Then he usually directs the worker to take some form of corrective action.

Under this set of circumstances, a supervisor will have

Exhibit 1. Feedback process typical of many work situations.

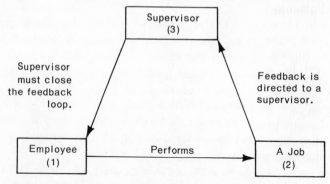

many more encounters with employees which involve negative feedback than positive feedback because so much of the supervisor's time is invested in running down problems.

The consequence of this feedback procedure is that the supervisor is placed in a situation of constantly being in a negative position relative to his employee. The "no news is good news" syndrome develops among the employees. The response to the question, "How do you know if you are doing a good job?" becomes, "Well, I haven't seen the foreman all day, so things must be going all right."

An alternative feedback process is providing the employee with the feedback through the same channels as the supervisor. In a bank or insurance company, this may mean channeling questions or complaints directly to the individual involved. Individual performance reports can be given to each employee on a regular basis. In manufacturing, providing the employee with lab reports or other data can be effective. Exhibit 2 illustrates this model.

When a problem comes up, the employee who performed the job should get the first opportunity to resolve it. It is when he or she proves ineffective at doing so that the supervisor should get involved. The definition of ineffectiveness varies by industry, but in all work situations it is possible to identify a set of parameters (which usually involves a time dimension and a magnitude dimension) within which employees can be considered to be performing with reasonable effectiveness.

Providing the employee with the opportunity for resolving negative feedback is important since without this opportunity, the job incumbent is not exercising control. Rather, direct feedback becomes only an intense source of reprisal.

Receiving direct feedback also puts the employee in a position to obtain a better qualitative feel for how the job is going and lessens the dependency relationship with his supervisor regarding positive feedback. The opportunity to receive direct, positive feedback can go a long way in meeting the achievement and recognition needs of employees. It is this relationship between feedback and need satisfaction which makes personal control so effective.

Providing the employee with direct feedback does not prevent the supervisor from receiving information on each employee, although the format through which this information is transmitted to the supervisor may change somewhat. For example, instead of being notified of each instance of negative feedback, a supervisor may receive daily, weekly, or monthly summaries on performance. Thus, the supervisor is monitoring trends, rather than getting involved in every problem situation. The supervisor may only get involved in problems of a particular magnitude, at which point consultation with the em-

Exhibit 2. Feedback system for personal control.

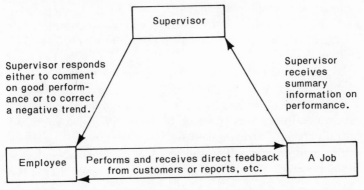

ployee is appropriate. Or he may monitor performance on a sample basis.

The supervisor's time is channeled toward involvement where it is needed most: on the most difficult problems or in overseeing the work of those employees whose performance indicates that they require more-direct supervision. In most operations, this latter group will be a distinct minority of the work force.

THE HUMAN RESOURCE MODEL AS BASIS FOR EVALUATING STRUCTURAL CHANGES

The human resource model is a set of assumptions and expectations about people and organizations which tend to lead to a distinct approach to the solution of people problems. Specifically, the model states that:

1. Most people desire to contribute in a meaningful way to the attainment of significant objectives.

2. The majority of workers are capable of doing so to a much greater extent than their present jobs require.

3. Management's basic task is the creation of a work situation which allows subordinates to contribute as broad a range of their talents as possible toward attaining organization goals.

4. As employees develop their skills, opportunities for personal control should be expanded.

5. Changes in the work situation which allow for greater utilization of employee capabilities will result in employees' exercising responsible self-direction and concentrating their energies on the attainment of significant organization objectives.[14]

Structural changes which allow employees to exercise their capabilities more fully—particularly in the areas of problem solving and contributing to the initiation of adjustments in the production process—will result in favorable behavioral and attitude changes. Structural changes which frustrate these capabilities will often result in dysfunctional behavioral and attitudinal change. The utilization of employee capabilities is the common denominator which determines whether a structural change will produce positive or negative employee behavior on the job.

How management structures the work situation, particularly with regard to efforts at control, is a crucial determinant of employee performance. But proper structuring of the work situation for human resource utilization is a multidimensional and difficult process. It involves examination of departmental organization, supervisory behavior, the technical organization of jobs, information flows, and even equipment design.

Further, other considerations, such as technical product problems and administrative issues, compete for management's attention. Chapter 3 begins to examine the elements and dimensions of successful managing through the structuring of the work situation itself.

REFERENCES

1. This definition of control emphasizes a particular aspect of the control process: the regulation of employee behavior. Some authors have called for a more precise definition of control, which refers specifically to the plan-do-observe-compare-correct cycle, which management regularly performs. However, a considerable amount of the activities which managers consider to be controls has to do with the direction and regulation of employee behavior. Further, this emphasis on regulating behavior is not, as we shall see, divorced from the process of planning, doing, observing, comparing, and correcting.

    For a formal review of the issues involved in the concept of control, see Giovanni B. Giglioni and Arthur G. Bedeian, "A Conspectus of Management Control Theory: 1900–1972," *Academy of Management Journal*, vol. 17, no. 2 (June 1974).

2. Douglas M. McGregor, *The Human Side of Enterprise* (New York: McGraw-Hill, 1960).

3. Michael Argyle, *The Social Psychology of Work* (Middlesex, England: Penguin Books, 1972), p. 96.

4. Ibid., p. 120.

5. See J. Stacy Adams, "Inequity in Social Exchange," in Leonard Berkowitz, ed., *Advances in Experimental Social Psychology*, 6 vols. (New York: Academic Press, 1964–1972), vol. 2, pp. 267–299. Both Argyle (Reference 3) and Lawler (*Motivation in Work Organizations*, Reference 10) offer discussions of Adams' theory.

6. J. S. Adams and W. B. Rosenbaum, "The Relationship of Worker Productivity to Cognitive Dissonance about Wage Inequities," *Journal of Appied Psychology*, vol. 46 (1962); J. S. Adams, "Productivity and Work Quality as a Function of Wage Inequities," *Industrial Relations*, 1963.

7. Abraham H. Maslow, *Motivation and Personality* (New York: Harper & Row, 1954).

8. Frederick Herzberg, Bernard Mausner, and Barbara B. Snyderman, *The Motivation to Work* (New York: John Wiley & Sons, 1959).

9. L. L. Cummings and A. M. El Salmi, "Empirical Research on the Basis and Correlates of Managerial Motivation: A Review of the Literature," *Psychological Bulletin*, vol. 70, pp. 127–144.

10. J. Richard Hackman and Edward E. Lawler, "Employee Reactions to Job Characteristics," *Journal of Applied Psychology*, vol. 55, no. 3 (June 1971); Edward E. Lawler, *Motivation in Work Organizations* (Monterey, Calif.: Brooks/Cole, 1973).

11. Arthur N. Turner and Paul R. Lawrence, *Industrial Jobs and the Worker* (Boston: Harvard Business School, 1965). Turner and Lawrence discovered a differing response pattern between workers in towns and cities in the relationship between task attributes and job satisfaction, a finding which focused considerable attention on cultural factors as intervening variables in job satisfaction research.

12. Jack E. Powers, "Job Enrichment: How One Company Overcame the Obstacles," *Personnel*, May–June 1972.

13. Richard E. Walton, "How to Counter Alienation in the Plant," *Harvard Business Review*, November–December 1972, p. 70.

14. This review of the human resource model is adapted from Raymond E. Miles, "Human Relations or Human Resources," *Harvard Business Review*, July–August 1965.

3

managing through the work itself

A crucial factor shaping organization structure at the point where employees relate to the organization is the organization's approach to control (regulation) of employee behavior.

If the organization responds to employee performance problems by implementing controls which frustrate employee capabilities, increased problems and resentment are predictable outcomes. These outcomes reinforce management's belief that organization controls are necessary. As a result, the organization increasingly comes to depend on organization controls.

On the other hand, if the organization responds to employee performance problems by assessing what, if any, structural characteristics are causing the problems, it is more likely to implement changes which build on employee capabilities. Improved employee performance is the predicted outcome, resulting in increased willingness by managers to consider similar changes in the future.

Exhibit 3 presents a schematic model of the relationship between controls, structure, and employee behavior. First, this exhibit illustrates that the basic point of intervention in correcting structurally caused performance problems should be

Exhibit 3. Relationship between structure, controls, and employee performance.

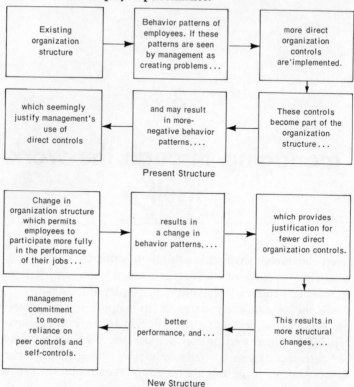

Present Structure

New Structure

those elements of structure which have to do with regulating behavior. Second, it shows the role which successful experience plays in initiating this type of change by encouraging additional efforts at structural change on the part of managers.

JOB DESIGN AS THE DETERMINANT OF THE EMPLOYEE'S ROLE

Organization structure, then, is a crucial determinant of employee performance. (The most fundamental aspect of organization structure affecting the individual employee is the design of his or her job.) The basic unit of all forms of social organization, including the business organization, is the prescribed roles which members fill.

A role is the set of behaviors, or actions, which other members of the organization expect an individual to perform. Many of these behaviors are explicitly spelled out in the form of rules, procedures, or laws. Others are implicitly communicated by the degree of approval or disapproval expressed by others. In formal organizations, job content and the manner in which that content is structured represent the individual's expected formal role and also represent the most persuasive influence on his total role within the organization.

How jobs are structured (1) communicates management's interpretation of a worker's abilities, (2) limits or encourages his or her participation in the solution of problems which confront the work unit, (3) determines how involved he or she is in the success of the operation, and (4) places limits on actual physical mobility. In short, it prescribes the experiences the employee will have while on the job.

Increasingly, it is becoming clear that job design involves more than analysis of task structure. While actual tasks are important, equally important is how those tasks are arranged. And even more important, the way in which work is distributed, the quality of feedback a job incumbent receives, and the action the incumbent is allowed to take in response to the feedback constitute a major part of the way in which the job is designed.

From the experience of several corporations, two distinct approaches to job design—job enrichment and team production —have evolved as successful ways of structuring work so that a full range of employee capabilities is utilized. (Team production is also referred to as "semi-autonomous work groups.") Much of this chapter will be devoted to examining job enrichment and team production as two distinct methods of managing through the work itself.

MODEL OF AN ENRICHED JOB

The parameters of a well-designed job have developed through the experience of those companies which implemented the basic principles of job enrichment. Job enrichment is a strategy for redesigning jobs to maximize their interest and challenge for the employee. In so doing, it strives to increase organizational effectiveness by getting the most out of the talents of individual employees.

Specifically, job enrichment attempts to provide the worker with a job which:

1. Is a complete piece of work in the sense that the worker can identify a series of tasks or activities which result in a definable product for a given receiver (client) or group of receivers.
2. Affords the employee as much decision-making control as possible over how he is to carry out that complete piece of work.
3. Provides direct feedback through the work itself on how well he is doing his job.[1]

These three dimensions define the parameters of any job. In so doing, they also define the limits of the individual's formal role within the organization.

Degree of Completeness

The first dimension of the model of an enriched job is the degree of completeness of the job. The completeness of a job has two aspects. First, to be complete, a job should be composed of a series of tasks which end with an identifiable result which is distinguishable from the results of other "pieces" of work. Another way of expressing this aspect of completeness is that a worker, after performing all those tasks, should be able to perceive a definite change in the product or service he is responsible for.

The second aspect of completeness is the client, or user, aspect. The job holder should be able to identify specific users or receivers of his work. Ideally, a complete job is one in which a given employee has a piece of work which is defined as certain logical activities for certain customers, and that piece of work should not be duplicated by anyone else in the work unit. For example, machine operators should channel their output to a specific set of operators at the next step of the production process, rather than having their output pooled and randomly distributed. Or underwriters in insurance companies should underwrite business for a specific set of agents rather than on a random work-flow basis.

Control Factor

The second dimension of a job is the control factor. A job incumbent should have as much decision-making control over how he is to perform his piece of work as possible. Given a certain level of competence, how much latitude is afforded the employee in how he accomplishes his job? Is the job holder permitted to deviate from prescribed methods and procedures in unusual situations or is he required to refer to a supervisor first? Such questions relate to the issue of employee control over his work.

Feedback

Finally, the third dimension of a job is feedback. An employee should frequently receive direct information on his work performance. Preferably, the feedback should not be dependent upon a supervisor, but should come from the work itself, through customer reactions, the immediate outcome of decisions, and performance criteria which go directly to the employee.

A complete piece of work, over which the employee has as much control as possible and through which he receives frequent, direct feedback on his performance—these dimensions have been identified from experience as being influential in affecting employee performance. As the work an individual is given to do approximates these dimensions, motivation and employee performance in most cases improves.

Exhibit 4. Example of enriched job for insurance coder.

A COMPLETE PIECE OF WORK

1. Unenriched work module.

Work is assigned within functions on a batch basis.

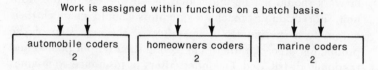

2. Enriched work module.

Work is assigned by insurance agency
(each coder is assigned a set of agencies).

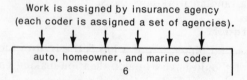

DECISION MAKING AND CONTROL

1. Coders decide which applications to work on first, based on knowledge of priorities.
2. Coders receive/direct any problems (such as system rejection) and try to solve the problem.
3. Agents are encouraged to phone coder on any information problems.

FEEDBACK

1. Direct phone contact is made with agents.
2. Mistakes are fed directly back.
3. Coder receives monthly printout on productivity, service times, and error rates for his/her work.

This three-part model of an enriched job is illustrated more fully in Exhibit 4.

Further Comments on the Model

First, it should be understood that the three dimensions are interdependent. To the extent that a job is incomplete (functionalized and/or fractionalized), it is difficult to allow for decision making which affects the job. Many supervisory jobs are mainly coordination functions between incomplete jobs.

Likewise, it is difficult to provide feedback on an incomplete piece of work. By the same token, feedback on a complete piece of work does not mean much to an individual who has had little say in the process of doing the job. Experience indicates that creating more complete jobs without providing employees the opportunity of exercising control does not result in either higher job satisfaction or improved performance.

And a person with both a complete piece of work and control over the work, but without regular and consistent feedback, is not likely to make good decisions. The point is that all three dimensions are equally important. And, further, the absence of any one of the three dimensions places crucial limitations on the development of the other two.

Second, the design of work is more than an engineering exercise in the traditional sense. While construction of a complete piece of work (dimension one) can be engineered, the other two dimensions require continual managing.

For example, the extent of the decisions and control a job incumbent is permitted to exercise should reflect his or her level of competence. Not all individuals are capable of the same levels of discretion. In any work unit a supervisor most likely has employees who vary considerably from one another regarding their ability to exercise discretion.

Too often what happens is that management determines the lowest level of capability it feels it can tolerate and sets procedures for everyone which reflect that level of ability. Under these conditions there is no reason to expect people to act responsibly. Indeed, what is communicated is that management expects them to act irresponsibly.

When management allows capable people to exercise discretion, what gets communicated is that management expects people to act responsibly. Individuals capably exercising discretion continue to enjoy autonomy and control over their work. The leverage point has been changed. The emphasis is on personal control.

As long as no one is permitted control over his work, acting responsibly is not an issue. However, when others have control over their jobs, an individual rarely wishes to be the only one requiring close supervision. Determining each individual's level of competence and encouraging further development are a basic task of supervision which can be accomplished in part through careful management of job structure.

Similarly, feedback can become a basis for job coaching on the part of the supervisor. The point is that within certain limits, the parameters of a job can be significantly managed to allow for individual development through basic task advancement.

Third, job redesign is a dynamic process. Although the three-part model is presented in static terms, in reality job structure is dynamic. Every time a product change, a supervisory change, a machine change, or a system change occurs, the content of jobs is affected. As will be discussed later, elements throughout the organization such as controller's requirements, data processing systems, wage and salary administration, to name just a few, are continually impacting upon jobs. These elements can either reinforce or not reinforce enriched job design. The point is that job design is not a one-time drive, but rather must be a continual organization process. Additionally, job changes do not occur in a vacuum, and other elements in the organization must be supportive of the concept.

JOB ENRICHMENT AS STRUCTURAL CHANGE

Unfortunately, in many companies, jobs are not structured in a way which approximates the three characteristics of an enriched job. Fragmentation, computerization, separation of doers from planners, and the notion that exact procedures are synonymous with control and coordination have resulted in the destruction of work. Through task combination, clear definition of who receives the work, placing power to act in the hands of the person doing the job, and feedback devices, job enrichment alters these organizational trends.

 Implementing job enrichment, then, obviously will require structural organizational change. An organization must be prepared to change procedures, methods of organizing work flow, and access to performance information. Job enrichment not only changes jobs horizontally (increasing the number of tasks a worker performs), but vertically as well (responsibility and authority now held by supervisors are built into the employees' jobs). Additionally, information channels are altered (feedback). Gradually, a new pattern of work relationships emerges as existing jobs are made more complete.

Before we continue further, it should be noted that task fragmentation, specialization, and the separation of the doers from planners in the design of jobs have not resulted from perversity on the part of managers or engineers. In a great many instances, these criteria rest on solid economic advantages in the production process. What is suggested here is that in many situations, within the constraints of technology and production requirements, more flexibility exists along the three dimensions of job design than is often recognized. Managing this flexibility can influence employee effectiveness on the job and is an important aspect of a manager's job.

Further, job design criteria which have been necessary in many mass production industries (such as specialization and functionalization in the assembly of mass-produced, complex products like automobiles) have been uncritically transferred to other industries with radically different technologies (such as insurance companies and service industries). Fundamental differences in the nature of the product and the process of production often limit the transferability of the advantages of job design criteria developed in the manufacturing industries to other business situations.

This issue will be explored further later on. For now, it should be recognized that technology and production volume are constraining factors in the design of jobs. Some technologies are more "enrichable" than others. One hundred percent correspondence with the model is not always possible. Sometimes adaptions prove effective; sometimes enrichment is just not feasible. However, inability to enrich all the way should not be an excuse out of hand for not making any improvements in job design.

Because job redesign involves structural organization change, the process through which the change is accomplished is a significant factor in the success or failure of a job enrichment effort. In fact, of the pitfalls which can arise during a job enrichment effort, just as many are attributable to the problem of organization change as to technical problems of job design. A considerable portion of subsequent chapters will deal with a process for effective structural organization change.

SOURCES OF EFFECTIVENESS OF ENRICHED JOB DESIGN

Enriched job design has proven effective in two fundamental ways. The first relates to the discussion of motivation in Chapter 2; that is, as jobs correspond to the model of an enriched job, it becomes possible for managers to provide employees with opportunities for experiencing achievement, recognition, competence, responsibility, task advancement, and other work-related feelings which are associated with motivation.

Experience suggests that many workers find jobs that are set up like the model more interesting and thus get more involved in their work. Especially in labor-intensive technologies, this increased involvement tends to translate into bottom-line savings through increased work pace, fewer errors, and more attention to production requirements.

The second has to do with economies of organization itself. In many operations, jobs which are redesigned to conform to the model allow for the realization of the following economies:

A decrease in internal transportation and handling time (the result of eliminating duplication of effort, such as two employees reviewing the same case history, etc.).

Elimination of down time of machinery while awaiting the arrival of a supervisor or specialist.

The advantage of a single individual's coordinating his own activities throughout his own job process (allowing for greater consistency in many instances).

The advantage of customers or users no longer being circulated from one function to another.

Most often these savings are realized in situations where the jobs were initially designed according to criteria effective for other technologies and purposes but inappropriate to the present one. These savings have contributed significantly to many of the dollar payouts which have been reported in the literature.

This fact has caused some overzealous critics of job enrichment to dismiss successful job enrichment efforts as "common sense." [2] If this is so, then a large number of jobs appear to have been set up with a distinct lack of common sense. It is argued here that it has not been a lack of common sense, but an attempt to transfer inappropriate job design criteria, which has resulted in these jobs being organized the way they are.

Let's examine each of the two sources of effectiveness, worker motivation and economies of organization, in closer detail.

Worker Motivation and Enriched Jobs

The previous chapters stressed the significance of a model of motivation in which achievement results in increased motivation rather than the reverse. Jobs which conform to the three-part model of an enriched job correspond to this theoretical ordering of events.

For example, setting up work on a client or receiver basis rather than on a functional basis provides opportunity for more direct feedback, both qualitative (direct receiver contact) and quantitative (computation of performance data on the basis of each employee's set of receivers). This feedback can directly provide achievement situations. So can tying the amount of discretion permitted any one individual to past performance on the job. When reliable performance on the job is rewarded with opportunities to exercise more control over one's job, the motivating influences of achievement and recognition are made operational.

Interviews with workers exposed to enrichment changes indicate that as jobs correspond to this model, the workers prefer the new structuring to the old. For example, consider this dialogue with an accounting clerk nine months after her job had been changed:

INTERVIEWER: *How do you receive your work?*

CLERK: I am responsible for a section of the alphabet, *D* through *G*. Any account whose last name falls in there is mine.

INTERVIEWER: *Has it always been this way?*

CLERK: No, our supervisor used to just give us a set number every day. It was changed to the new way last spring.

INTERVIEWER: *Which way is better?*

CLERK: I think this way.

INTERVIEWER: *Why?*

CLERK: Well, you know you are responsible for this section, so you try to get it right. Also, if a problem comes up, you don't have to figure out someone else's work; you know what you did.

Another clerk in the same office said, "You feel more responsible this way. If a mistake is made, you did it." Another commented, "Your work is your own."

In another office where considerable task combination had occurred, a worker commented that she enjoyed learning the new task. She had never realized all that was involved in processing a piece of work. In particular, she had never realized what kinds of problems other people ran into as a result of the tasks that she had been doing on her previous job.

In a manufacturing plant, the following interview with a machine operator occurred:

INTERVIEWER: *Lately, you have been keeping a record of breakdowns on your machines. Is that worthwhile?*

OPERATOR: Yes, I have learned a lot about these machines which surprised me. For example, number 7 is

INTERVIEWER: down more than three times [as often as] the
other machines. I never realized it was giving
me that many problems!

INTERVIEWER: *Anything else?*

OPERATOR: Well, the foreman, the mechanics, and I go
over the records each Friday and pinpoint the
problems. Then the mechanic lets me know
when he thinks he has corrected them. It seems
we are working together more. They seem to
be more interested in what is happening, and
we are on top of things.

Taken individually, these comments are anecdotal. Given as
representative of many such conversations, they are part of a
data pattern which suggests more involvement in the job as a
result of making the jobs correspond more closely to the three-
part model presented above. It should be noted that none of
these workers felt they were in a state of Utopian bliss. They
still had their ups and downs, but they were involved and
interested in their jobs, and this involvement was reflected in
improved turnover, absenteeism, and production data.

The model of an enriched job presented above has evolved
out of applied experience, but it corresponds closely to the
factors identified by research psychologists as important elements in work which satisfies higher-order needs. In summariz-
ing existing research, Edward Lawler advances the following
three criteria as being important to job satisfaction. The job
must:

1. Allow the worker to feel personally responsible for a
   meaningful portion of his work.
2. Involve doing something that is intrinsically meaningful
   or that is experienced as worthwhile to the individual.
3. Provide feedback about what is accomplished.[3]

Hackman and Lawler have identified variety, autonomy,
task identity, and feedback as core dimensions of meaningful
work.[4] Arthur Turner and Paul Lawrence previously produced

similar results on these core dimensions.[5] The task identity and variety measures in these studies roughly correspond to the first part of our model, although not completely. Autonomy is somewhat similar to the second part of the model. And, of course, feedback.

In summary, both practical experience and research suggest jobs become more meaningful when they are designed to fit the general criteria of the whole model.

Economies of Organization

Many of the savings reported from job enrichment are the result of economies of organization: Enriched job design actually allows more efficient operation of the work unit. Some observers note that such results are not truly attributable to enrichment since the savings accrue from "better engineering" of the jobs rather than more motivated workers working harder. There is an element of truth in this criticism, since it is sometimes implied in reports that the savings are solely the result of more satisfied workers working harder.

Two factors relative to this criticism must be recognized, however. First, a considerable amount of data indicates the workers do like the jobs better. Interviews and reliable questionnaires (in some instances administered as long as two years after the job design changes have been implemented) indicate higher levels of job satisfaction than existed before enriched job design. Thus, it appears that at least for some production technologies, effective production and satisfying work are not as diametrically opposed as managers have often assumed.

Second, improved motivation of employees does contribute to the realization of the savings, since opportunities for slacking abound in most of these situations. Indeed, one of the arguments often heard from managers in support of job fragmentation is that it is easier to police the activity of each employee. The dollar savings would remain only potential savings were employees not concerned with doing the work properly.

At least six sources of economies can be identified through a review of successful job enrichment implementations:

1. *Reduced down time.* Many enrichment-oriented changes allow a worker to make adjustments in equipment or machinery without prior consultation with a supervisor. For example, machine tenders are allowed to vary a machine speed in order to make some adjustment on the machine. Or operators shut down a machine and perform minor maintenance themselves. Or an employee calls for information direct from another department without going through a foreman. Once qualified, workers can perform these tasks most effectively, yet they are not permitted to do so in many shops.

Bennie Butts, an industrial engineer in the textile industry, illustrated the source of these savings most graphically for me. Production problems are first observed on the shop floor, most often by a worker. If the worker can make the correction himself, the control loop can be closed immediately. Down time or amount of second-quality product is held to a minimum. However, the higher up in hierarchy the right to authorize a correction rests, the longer the response time and the more units of production lost.

2. *Improved information on production.* In analyzing the work for sources of feedback, sometimes new measurements are initiated which previously did not exist. For example, a worker may begin recording machine problems and, along with a maintenance man, monitor performance of his machines on a weekly basis. This new measure may reveal problems with specific machines which were not previously apparent to management. This results in correction of the problem and therefore in more production.

A home-office clerk in an insurance company may keep his or her own policies status report, which gets mailed weekly to the field offices. This results in fewer queries on the policies in the first place and, second, in more rapid response to questions which are received.

Thus, creating formal feedback measures not only provides opportunities to measure achievement but may also produce information relevant to performance which previously was not available. This information can lead to improvements in technical organization.

3. *Centering work around the basic function or mission of the department.* Current job redesign technology centers around a systems approach to job design. As will be seen in later chapters, a central part of the design process is identifica- tion of key tasks for achieving the basic mission of the work unit.

In paper processing situations, this quite often results in the clustering into one job crucial tasks which were previously fragmented. This in turn results in a single individual's having control over a work item or knowledge of its whereabouts at all times. In situations where an item is awaiting additional information, there is a reduction in time spent both in matching mail to cases and in searching for items in response to customer questions.

4. *Direct user contact.* Setting up work on a user or client basis often results in direct communication between the receiver of the work and the person doing the work. Complaints, questions, and adjustments can often be accomplished without the intervention of a third party, such as a supervisor. This reduces communication problems which emerge when a person attempting to resolve the problem is not the person most familiar with the work.

This advantage tends to be realized in white collar or craft jobs. However, manufacturing operations have also benefited, such as when machine operators in two different departments are allowed to communicate directly with one another about production problems they have in common.

5. *Reduced start-up time on recycled cases.* In clerical and service jobs, the way a particular case has been handled may result in its being channeled back to the clerical or service department that originally dealt with it. Setting up work on a client basis will result in the recycling of the case to the same individual who handled it the first time around. That employee will require less time to become familiar with the particular situation than another person, who would be seeing the case for the first time.

Obviously, in those organizations in which a second employee takes over a case that has not been successfully completed, he must (1) become familiar with the basic situation, (2) figure out what action the first employee initiated and why, and (3) decide on a different course of action the second time around. This process usually takes time that could be saved if the original employee rehandled the case.

6. *Elimination of checkers, expeditors, and other special jobs.* One of the changes which usually accompany efforts at setting up jobs to correspond to the three-part model of an enriched job is that checking or inspection functions and expeditor functions get built into the jobs of the employees doing the actual production work. The employee responsible for performing a given piece of work is made responsible for inspecting it. In those situations where the work is regularly checked by other employees, this combination of responsibilities will result in reduced overhead due to the eliminated functions.

Each of the previous six factors represents a source of savings which have resulted from enriched job design. While they are not obtainable in all work situations, such savings can often be realized, particularly in clerical, administrative, and traditional machine-to-machine production shops.

The six factors especially illustrate the dangers of copying the assembly line as a generalized model of efficient work design. Assembly lines have proven efficient for producing automobiles, but the line foreman does not have to worry about matching different pieces of the car arriving in the mail or answering salesmen's questions about the current status of a specific car which may be buried under a stack of other cars. Such are the problems of the policy-changes-unit supervisor in a life insurance company. Different technologies place different sets of constraints on the organization of work.

TEAM PRODUCTION (SEMI-AUTONOMOUS WORK GROUPS)

An approach to work structuring which is different from job enrichment as we have been discussing it, is team production, or semi-autonomous work groups. In this approach, groups of workers are identified and assigned collective responsibility for successful completion of a segment of the production process.[6]

Typically, the teams will range in size from 5 to 15 employees. Usually, groups of this size are large enough to staff natural segments of the production process, yet small enough to allow for group identity and face-to-face interaction.

As a group, workers assume responsibility for making individual assignments for the necessary jobs, covering for absent group members, coping with production problems, counseling and coaching team members who are performing below standard, and selecting replacements for departing group members.

In addition to basic production work, the group performs such staff support functions as minor maintenance work, quality control, basic industrial engineering, and so forth. It receives basic management decision information such as costs, yields, deadlines, and company procedures. In effect, the group is collectively given an enriched job.

As with classical job enrichment, the process of implementing the team production concept is a crucial factor for success. In particular, considerable planning must be given to how the groups are to relate to the remainder of the corporation. For example, most companies implementing the concept to any great extent have made alterations in their compensation structure to reinforce the group concept. Usually, pay rate must be less directly tied to specific tasks performed and more directly tied to the range of skills which potentially an employee can perform.

JOB ENRICHMENT AND TEAM PRODUCTION COMPARED

Job enrichment and autonomous work groups share the beliefs that the design of work is an important element in employee motivation, that workers are capable of exercising personal control, and that opportunities to participate more fully in the production process will be met with a positive response by most workers. However, despite those common beliefs, they represent two distinct approaches to the structuring of work.

Presently, there are no data which allow for comparison of the relative merits of each approach. Nor, unfortunately, is our knowledge sophisticated enough to identify general categories of production technologies where one approach may be more appropriate than the other. It does appear that of the two, job enrichment is more compatible with the traditional hierarchical form of organization structure typical of virtually all business organizations today.

A company committed to implementing team production on a broad scale would, it appears, have to begin altering its structure much more to the designs of "industrial democracy," with the establishment of worker committees at all levels of the hierarchy and less emphasis on the prerogatives of management. However, over the long run, pressure from society may well dictate considerable alteration in our contemporary hierarchical forms of organization structure.

A basic distinction between job enrichment and team production is the emphasis the former places on individual psychology and personal control, while the latter emphasizes social relationships and group control. However, both recognize the importance of each category of control.

For example, in job enrichment, as individuals within the work unit assume more responsibility, the group norm for performance rises, putting an element of social pressure on others to accept more responsibility for their jobs. Conversely, in team production, emphasis is placed on the creation of task assignments which are as broad as possible and allow for the exercising of individual judgment.

As will be seen later, the two strategies confront different kinds of problems which must be overcome during the implementation process. This is to be expected of two approaches which result in basically different forms of work unit organization: In job enrichment a work unit is designed on a natural (client or individual) basis, reporting through a traditional supervisor who deals with each employee individually. On the other hand, the team approach is designed to provide much flexibility and rotation within the team, which usually reports to management through a team leader or representative.

BEYOND THE DESIGN OF JOBS

The solutions to many performance problems require structural changes which go beyond the design of individual jobs within a given work unit. Often tasks or functions need to be moved across department lines. Sometimes, these tasks are built into existing jobs as part of a job redesign effort; sometimes new jobs are created which interface closely with existing jobs.

For example, conflict between operations and maintenance is common to manufacturing plants. Operations is continually after maintenance to make machine adjustments and repairs on equipment. Maintenance is trying to keep on top of required maintenance schedules.

Many times the solution is to identify simple and recurring repairs and adjustments and include these in the operator's job. In this way, operators have a more complete job with additional control since they can now make these repairs and adjustments. Thus, machine down time is usually reduced. At the same time, maintenance men are able to concentrate on their primary responsibility, performing major repair work and machine overhauls. Improved levels of maintenance usually result. Additionally, a source of conflict has been structurally removed.

A potential alternative solution involves having operators and maintenance men report to the same foreman and assigning maintenance men a specific set of operators to service (this creates a customer relationship). Under these combined structural changes, operators and maintenance men tend to work more cohesively.

In white collar operations accounting clerks often are dependent on information from other clerks in the office, and the accounting clerks spend much time clarifying information. Sometimes it is possible to combine the two jobs. If different skill requirements prevent this, it may be possible to move the accounting clerks into the other clerical unit. If work is assigned on a client basis, the two sets of clerks can have largely overlapping assignments, which will provide them with the opportunity to work closely together.

The foregoing examples illustrate the need for managers to consider a broader range of structural issues in relation to performance problems than solely the design of individual jobs. Many times the manner in which a plant or office is structured contributes to dysfunctional employee behavior. How entire functions are expected to interface with each other, how plants or offices fit into the larger organization structure, and how job mobility ladders within the plant or office are organized can create pressures which result in performance difficulties.

For example, in the case of the large metropolitan utility discussed in Chapter 1, the fact that an operator's mobility ladder included working as a member of maintenance teams for extended periods of time contributed to the operator transfer problem.

There is, of course, a close relationship between how jobs are structured and the way the larger plant or office is organized. Sometimes solving problems at one level requires dealing with both.

Given acceptance of the need for restructuring for better utilization of human resources, the problem arises as to how. What are the basic elements of a successful restructuring effort? Part Two outlines an action model for implementing a successful structural change effort.

REFERENCES

1. This model of an enriched job was developed by David A. Whitsett. See Whitsett, "The Enriched Job," *Personnel Administrator*, September–October 1972.

2. Mitchell Fein, "Job Enrichment: A Re-evaluation," *Sloan Management Review*, winter 1974.

3. Edward E. Lawler, *Motivation in Work Organizations* (Monterey, Calif.: Brooks/Cole, 1973).

4. J. Richard Hackman and Edward E. Lawler, "Employee Reactions to Job Characteristics," *Journal of Applied Psychology*, vol. 55 (1971).

5. Arthur Turner and Paul Lawrence, *Industrial Jobs and the Worker* (Cambridge, Mass.: Harvard Business School, 1965).

6. A detailed account of an application of this approach can be found in Richard E. Walton, "How to Counter Alienation in the Plant," *Harvard Business Review*, November–December 1972.

part two

restructuring
work

Job enrichment affects the most basic interface between
the employee and the organization: the design of the job
the employee is given to do. Job design determines the
individual employee's role within the organization, can
significantly affect the motivation to perform well, and to
a great extent determines the compensation, status, and
other benefits an employee receives from the organization.

In short, individual jobs are a basic element in the
structure of an organization. It is appropriate, therefore,
that the design of jobs be the central part of any strategy
for structural organization development.

Many organizations are not presently operating in a
manner conducive to enriched job design. How then can
job enrichment be introduced so that it gradually becomes
a viable management strategy within the organization?
Part Two explores the elements of successful organization
change in the way work is structured. Chapters 4 through

7 concern themselves with presenting a model for effectively implementing job enrichment in a work organization. Chapter 8 deals with team approaches to job design.

While the change models presented in Part Two are directed toward the redesign of work, many of the problems confronted in redesigning work are characteristic of organization change in general. Therefore, the reader should consider the basic approach suggested as applicable to a wide range of change-directed activities.

4

the job enrichment specialist
as a change agent

Experience has proven that the *process* through which job enrichment is introduced into an organization has a significant influence on the results achieved. If the implementation process is not properly controlled, failure is a predictable outcome. This chapter discusses two characteristics of successful job enrichment implementation: the role of the job enrichment specialist as a change agent and the importance of the departmental key man to an enrichment effort.

THE JOB ENRICHMENT SPECIALIST

When a company first becomes involved in job enrichment, its goal should be the development of an internal consulting capacity. Among the advantages of such an approach is that it builds expertise in job enrichment into the organization on a permanent basis and aids in coordinating the effort to the best advantage of the company.

Throughout this book the term "job enrichment specialist" is used to describe an internal staff consultant charged with assisting management in the development and implementation of job redesign strategies. However, this specialist must acquire consulting skills beyond traditional job enrichment. As will become clear in later chapters, he or she must be capable of performing as a broad-based human resource consultant and should define his or her role in those terms. For example, the job enrichment specialist will need to be capable of helping managers determine if team production technologies are practical and when job enrichment is not feasible. He or she must also be capable of developing and implementing achievement-oriented management development activities, of helping to re-design organization control systems, and of developing team-work between managers at different levels in the corporate hierarchy, to name some of the necessary skills.

Development of this range of skills takes time. However, in those corporations with effective job restructuring efforts, the internal staff specialists have striven to develop a wide range of competence as organizational consultants.

Three characteristics tend to be true of the effective internal job enrichment specialist:

1. He (or she) needs to really believe that most people do want to do a good job if the work is structured in a way which allows them to do so. That is, he needs to personally believe the fundamental assumptions on which job enrichment rests. If not, he will not be persuasive on crucial points.

2. He needs to be credible in the eyes of managers. His experience in business must be such that he commands the confidence of managers with whom he must work. He should be capable of convincing people that his suggestions should be given a chance.

3. He needs to have verbal skills which are effective in group situations and meetings.

Given these characteristics, good internal job enrichment consultants have operated out of personnel, industrial engineering, and systems departments, to name the most typical bases of operation.

Job enrichment is not something which can be accomplished as a side project. The specialist must devote his time to learning from a broad variety of experiences in applying the concept, be available when needed by client departments, and integrate job enrichment with other manpower utilization and organization development techniques. In short, job enrichment is a full-time job.

Of critical importance is the model on which the specialist bases his behavior. If first-line supervision is to carry out the enrichment process to its fullest potential, it will require technical support beyond a basic training workshop. This factor dictates a basic characteristic of a successful job enrichment effort. A job enrichment effort should be designed on a consultative model rather than a training model. In other words, the job enrichment specialist should be prepared to function as consultant to managers regarding the feasibility and appropriateness of job enrichment changes as opposed to serving primarily as a teacher of job enrichment principles.

THE CONSULTING VERSUS THE TRAINING MODEL

The distinction between consulting and training may at first glance appear to be trivial. However, in practice, the subtle differences which distinguish the consulting relationship from a training relationship emerge as most important. Four basic dimensions along which the activities of a consultant differ from those of a trainer can be identified: (1) approach to the larger organization, (2) relationship to managers and supervisors, (3) type of expertise, and (4) involvement in the change process. Table 1 presents a summary of the differences between the training and consulting models with regard to these dimensions.

As can readily be seen from Table 1, the consulting model requires fundamentally different behavior from the job enrichment expert than would be the case were he to view himself as a trainer. The consulting model assumes that the job enrichment specialist is a catalyst for change. As such, his activities must be directed toward creating an organizational climate which facilitates change.

Table 1. Differences between the training and consulting
relationships.

Basic Dimension	Training Model	Consulting Model
Approach to the larger organization.	Enters at any point to fill a specific training need.	Gains confidence of upper management as an agent for shaping long-range changes.
Relationship to managers and supervisors.	Detached, with only sporadic and limited association.	Works on a regular basis to help solve operating problems.
Type of expertise.	Skilled in various instructional methods.	Skilled in analyzing organizational dynamics.
Involvement in the change process.	A teacher of basic principles and procedures.	An active catalyst for change and involved in influencing the outcome.

This perspective has profound implications for the entire job enrichment process. It influences the professional qualifications of the job enrichment specialist, how he enters the client organization, the type of relationship he builds with line managers, and the objectives and controls he establishes for the job enrichment effort. For example, a job enrichment effort constructed on the consulting model would require that the specialist not only have a knowledge of basic job enrichment principles, but also a good understanding of organization dynamics and experience in guiding change. Additionally, he must establish credibility with managers as representing a resource which can help solve operating problems, rather than as an instructor of procedures.

Conversely, trainers assume little responsibility for *direct* initiation of change. Their principal objective is the transference of a specific set of skills, be it technical, managerial, or whatever. Proper application of these skills once the trainee is removed from the training situation is peripheral to the trainer's area of responsibility.

At this point, an obvious question arises: Why construct a job enrichment program on the consulting model when it is obviously more involved and requires of the organization a greater investment in time, money, and effort than the more conventional training approach? Before proceeding further, it is appropriate to address this question.

THE NEED FOR A CONSULTIVE MODEL

As a vehicle for employee and management development, training is misused by too many companies. They are committed to seminars or workshops but fail to distinguish whether the training offered is applicable for the people receiving it. Visit any number of corporations noted for their progressive management development programs and what you are likely to find is supervisors and managers at all levels attending seminars in management and business practices. The firms seldom optimize the benefits which can be derived from such activity because of lack of opportunities for participants to meaningfully employ their newly developed skills.

Consider the Tennessee utility company experience described in Chapter 1. The company failed to realize any meaningful payoff from the customer relations course because management considered its problem to be a matter of employee development and failed to recognize the company had an obligation to create a situation where workers could apply their new skills. It was content to base its evaluations of the seminar on employee comments, rather than looking for objective results.

Had management been results-oriented, it would have recognized that employees returned to the same work structure as before the seminar, one which restricted their opportunity to perform. Not only did performance not improve, but in some instances, morale was lowered in workers who recognized that there was a better way of doing things.

Another example involves a major corporation which regularly conducts an intensive two-week conference for managers being groomed for high positions. For ten days the participants study financial, systems, and manpower development techniques. Homework often keeps the midnight oil burning into the dawn hours.

In short, the course work is high-powered and the managers return to their jobs enthusiastic to apply what they have learned. A year later the turnover rate for participants is almost 50 percent. The company returns the men to the old structure to await promotion. Many of the better ones grow restless and seek opportunities elsewhere.

The lesson is simple and direct: Train for a specific purpose. Underutilization of talent is a major source of employee frustration. In the case of job enrichment, supervisors are trained to make changes in the work structure. If they return from a workshop prepared to make changes and confront opposition from their superiors, demoralization of first-line supervision is a potential result.

It is the responsibility of the job enrichment specialist to create a situation in which supervisors and managers can effectively deal with their superiors. Before initiating the training program, the specialist should develop rapport with upper management so that it supports the intentions of managers and supervisors. He needs to aid supervisors in identifying and analyzing the possible pitfalls of their proposed changes and suggest ways of overcoming them.

In other words, the job enrichment specialist must structure a situation which allows supervisors to apply job enrichment principles after they have been instructed in the techniques. If he fails to do this, little meaningful change will result. Experience indicates that in the case of job enrichment, training alone is insufficient to initiate the change process.

In one company where the job enrichment effort is on a strict training model, managers and supervisors are put through a five-day training package in job enrichment and sent back to their units without any follow-up. The instructors pridefully point to letters from managers bearing testimonial to the course and an occasional instance of a success story.

However, that company has not begun to realize the true

potential of job enrichment. While participants leave the training program with a good understanding of job enrichment concepts and some ideas they want to implement, they seldom get an opportunity to apply their knowledge in a significant way. Meaningful organization change is a complex process, and many potential pitfalls confront the first-line supervisor attempting to implement job enrichment on his own. The consulting role of the job enrichment specialist should provide a vehicle which helps the first-line supervisor to implement the change process.

The following two case studies illustrate the importance of the consulting role. In both cases, managers and supervisors participated in a three-day training workshop. It was evident from their behavior and comments in the workshop that they accepted the concept of job enrichment as a managerial technique.

Case one involved a clerical unit in a financial services company. The unit was located in a field office several hundred miles from the home office. During the workshop, the managers and supervisors had devised the list of initial job changes they wanted to make, but the target date for beginning implementation passed without any activity. A month later no items had been implemented.

A return visit to the field office revealed the cause of the delay. The supervisors had become bogged down in trying to decide how to begin. The changes they wished to make required that many of the clerks be thoroughly cross-trained. This led to the supervisors' becoming more involved in personalities than they had been at the workshop. The more they thought about the individuals involved, the less confident they became about making changes. Further, the office was below productivity standards, and this made the managers more uneasy about making any changes.

The problem here is often encountered in job enrichment efforts: Management becomes preoccupied with the negative characteristics of present employee behavior rather than orienting itself to the positive elements which could improve performance in the future. The specialist's first order of business was to redirect management's attention. The managers and supervisors needed to concentrate their energies on building better jobs for the good performers, rather than focusing their concern on the nonproducers.

This approach promised to pay off from two perspectives. First, building better jobs for the producers offered the opportunity to capitalize upon the abilities of the best employees instead of restricting their potential output. Allowing better workers to perform a more complete unit of work would increase their impact on the system.

Second, by selectively giving the better people qualitatively improved jobs, management would create a situation which would afford marginal producers a concrete reason for improving their performance. As long as poor performers do the same tasks as good performers, the reward system reinforces those attitudes it was created to combat.

After some discussion with the specialist, management agreed to introduce job content changes on a selective basis. Those clerks who supervisors felt were capable of performing a more complete unit of work no longer received their work on a batch basis. Rather, they were given responsibility for the total clerical function of certain accounts.

Accounts were assigned so that each employee processed the same amount of work as she had before the change, but now she was responsible for the quality of service each account received on a continuing basis. In addition, the clerks were responsible for handling any problems which involved clerical service on their accounts. Previously, clerical problems had been handled by the supervisors.

The results were interesting. Clerks with responsibility for total accounts rapidly became familiar with the history of each account. It was possible for them to monitor the quality of service a customer received and they were able to set priorities in their work schedule. After three months, the percentage of errors dropped and complaints from accounts handled by a specific clerk were negligible. Further, productivity, as measured by volume of work processed, was consistently higher for the clerks working on a total account basis.

Three weeks after the changes had been made, two clerks not involved in the initial implementation requested to be put on the new system. After some consultation by the supervisor as to what was required, they were allowed to switch. Within six months, 90 percent of the clerical unit was either on the new system or training toward it.

Had it not been for the specialist's follow-up, probably few results would have been obtained from the supervisors' participation in training session. Back on the job, they would have convinced themselves that such far-reaching changes were not possible with their employees. However, the follow-up on the part of the specialist kept the discussion going, and he was able to convince the supervisors to initiate a modest change effort.

Once the hurdle of making the first changes was overcome and the supervisors had obtained some concrete results, their enthusiasm and commitment to job enrichment became personalized. Indeed, the specialist had to caution the supervisors to contain their enthusiasm, to be sure (1) that they thought through thoroughly each of the additional changes they wished to make and (2) that they did not lose control of their units by implementing far-reaching changes too rapidly.

Our second case also involves a rather large clerical operation, this time in the credit department of a bank. Within a month after the training workshop, the manager and service supervisors implemented a series of enrichment-oriented changes. The items were not very ambitious and it was questionable whether they would have an effect.

An interesting situation developed. The clerks responded to the changes in an extremely positive fashion. As a result, the service supervisors became enthusiastic about making additional changes and began to see realistic possibilities for improving the quality of service. Although supportive, the manager was hesitant to let the supervisors continue the change process. The supervisors began to feel frustrated over their lack of authority to act.

Once again, this situation is typical of the implementation process. Success reinforces front-line supervision's confidence in job enrichment, and it begins to see potential for improved performance of which it was previously unaware. However, the department manager, further removed from the production process, remained concerned about losing control.

In this situation, the best response is to address this legitimate fear on the part of the manager in a direct, but constructive way. One of the fastest ways to blow up a business operation is to let subordinates innovate without direction or control. A quick assessment of the manager's situation revealed that his conservativeness was well founded. In addition to the clerical unit, he was responsible for an administrative operation which was also part of the credit department. This responsibility occupied a considerable portion of his time. Thus, he felt that he was not as current on things in the clerical unit as he would have liked to be. Also, once before he delegated some of his authority with near disastrous results.

A detailed discussion ensued between the manager and the specialist as to what kind of information the manager should be seeing on a regular basis in order to be more current on what was happening in the clerical operation. The parameters which should define the limits of supervisors' authority and methods to insure that these parameters were not violated were explored. In all, three two-hour discussions on feedback and control took place. During these meetings, the results of the initial changes were emphasized.

By the fourth meeting the manager was willing to give responsibility for implementing minor job enrichment changes to the supervisors on the condition that he be informed of all changes. Supervisors were also given responsibility for isolating and writing up items which required his further consideration. The result was that supervisors had more flexibility in handling the units. For the first time, they were able to respond to problems as front-line managers rather than as clerks. This took some additional pressure off the manager. It also streamlined the job enrichment process and resulted in significant gains in unit performance. In time, the manager became more comfortable with letting his supervisors manage. Once again, the job enrichment specialist, acting as an internal consultant, was able to overcome an apparent roadblock in the enrichment process and enable the process to continue to evolve.

In both of the above instances, the full payoff of the process was only realized after an intervention on the part of the job enrichment specialist. It is difficult to overemphasize the consulting aspect of the specialist's role. In almost every instance, it is possible to predict that no matter how enthusiastic managers are about the job enrichment concept at the workshop, they are going to require additional help if significant performance gains are to be realized. At this time, it will be useful to cite five of the more common obstacles or pitfalls which the job enrichment specialist needs to help first-line supervision overcome.

FIVE PITFALLS COMMON TO THE
IMPLEMENTATION PROCESS

As discussed above, one pitfall is resistance from superiors. In many companies, responsibility for work procedures lies several levels above first-line supervision. Despite lip service to the contrary, meaningful change in the way work is done usually requires approval from a regional manager and often even a vice president. The manager who, following a training session in job enrichment, tries to gain approval for work changes typically receives encouragement for his efforts, but not approval. Removed as they are from the immediate situation, his superiors are not thinking along the same lines. The result can be a demoralized manager.

A second source of failure is the tendency for managers to underrate the abilities of the people they have working for them. Thus, they hesitate to make changes with an impact. One of the basic premises of job enrichment is that often the work structure gives little incentive for exhibiting good work habits.

The great majority of workers respond positively to an improved work structure. At the training workshop, first-line supervision typically becomes enthusiastic over the logic of this idea. However, back on the firing line, confronted once more with production deadlines and personnel problems, it is natural for them to become less convinced of the workability of job enrichment in their own situations. The result is too often a watered-down effort.

A third pitfall is the inability of the first-line supervision to find the time to meet for planning changes. Once back on the job, they find themselves too busy fighting fires to take the time to plan job enrichment changes. The supervisors put off planning and implementing until "I get more time." Of course, more time seldom becomes available, and the longer they procrastinate, the less chance there is that the company will reap tangible results from the investment in training.

Sometimes first-line supervision underestimates the influence it has with superiors and thus becomes too unambitious. It doesn't pursue changes for fear of being "shot down." A fifth pitfall is supervisors' not having the backup support to implement effectively, including training aids and access to crucial information (production projections, planned product changes, and the like).

The important point is that the training model does not provide effective vehicles for overcoming the pitfalls, whereas the job enrichment specialist working on the consultive model assumes continuing responsibility for structuring a successful implementation effort. For example, if the specialist is successful in gaining the confidence of upper management in a department or division, he is in a position to help lower supervision overcome resistance from above. In fact, if the specialist has properly laid pre-implementation groundwork, resistance may not emerge at all.

With regard to the tendency for managers to underrate the abilities of their employees, by working with managers on a regular basis, the specialist can repeatedly help managers try to understand the underlying motives of employment behavior. Similarly, the continuing involvement of the specialist often is enough to keep the problem of procrastination from arising.

In sum, by helping supervisors deal with upper management, providing continuing technical expertise, prodding supervisors into action and being generally supportive on a continuing basis, the specialist creates a context for which training in job enrichment principles is a meaningful experience for managers and supervisors. Through being actively concerned with the process of implementation as well as with theory and technique, the job enrichment specialist creates a role for himself as a vehicle for overcoming possible pitfalls. Such a role extends itself considerably beyond the traditional training function being practiced in many companies.

While discussing the value of the consulting model, it is important to call attention to an additional characteristic of the job enrichment process which is facilitated by the consulting relationship. Although results from job enrichment are derived from the changing structure of work which employees are asked to perform, the ingenuity and creativity which emerge in a manager's style as a result of applying job enrichment techniques are what maintains the effort after the specialist withdraws. The source of the changes needs to be the managers and supervisors of the line organization itself, rather than being arbitrarily imposed by the specialist.

The process of implementation which is emerging for effecting job enrichment changes emphasizes management involvement in the planning and organization of work. Only if this is true will the company have developed an organization which is capable of dealing with demands for change on a continuing basis.

In this sense, job enrichment is a technique of structurally oriented management development. While the desired result of implementing job enrichment is improved employee performance as a result of changes in the work structure, the *process* of implementing job enrichment is in every sense an

Exhibit 5. Various results of job enrichment implementation.

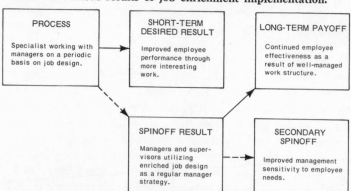

exercise in management development. A hoped for spinoff of the implementation process is a more capable team of managers who regularly utilize job design as a management strategy (see Exhibit 5).

It is in the development of managers and supervisors as effective designers of jobs that long-term benefits of implementing job enrichment are realized by the organization. These long-term benefits are best realized through a consulting relationship.

When designing a job enrichment implementation, the emphasis is on gaining first-line management support. The job enrichment specialist does not make changes in the jobs; he serves only as a resource. While he makes suggestions and must try to convince managers to be aggressive in restructuring work, final responsibility for the changes rests with line supervision.

Although the job enrichment specialist will want to confer with supervisors on a regular basis, ownership of the job enrichment effort must always be identified as being with line supervision. The specialist should avoid intensive involvement with any one client department and try to accomplish his objectives in a minimum amount of time.

If the job enrichment specialist is to accomplish this objective of being an effective catalytic change agent, selection of a primary contact within the department (key man) is a crucial issue.

THE DEPARTMENTAL KEY MAN CONCEPT

One of the buzzwords which has been part of the job enrichment literature since Robert Ford published his account of the Bell System's program is the key man.* Traditionally, writers on job enrichment have employed the concept of the key man to refer to an individual from a client department who is assigned to work closely with the job enrichment specialist. The intent is for the specialist to train the key man in job enrichment techniques so that after an effort gets under way, the specialist can withdraw from the department.

Proper selection of the key man has proven to be an influential factor in the outcome of a job enrichment program. However the definition of the key man concept here is something other than that described in the early literature. There is little point in attempting to convert the key man into a job enrichment specialist. Rather, the key man should be a *coordinator* of the job enrichment effort in the client department.

In the key man, the job enrichment specialist needs an individual whose position and experience counterbalance the specialist's weaknesses and inadequacies. No matter how close a relationship develops between the line organization and the job enrichment specialist, the specialist still must deal with the reality that he is an outsider. He is in a staff relationship and bears no responsibility for the operation of the client department.

As such, the specialist must deal with the difficulties which are inherent in line-staff relationships. Jealousy by line supervisors of their prerogatives, concern over who receives credit for successes, the need to influence without formal authority to direct, and continual shifts in the extent to which each party

* *Motivation through the Work Itself* (New York: American Management Associations, 1969).

sees himself as dependent on the other are but a small sample of such tension-creating difficulties.

An important function of the departmental key man is making sure that they do not evolve into major hindrances to the implementation effort. If the key man role is modeled after the specialist and evolves into an internal departmental staff position, it is unlikely that the key man will be able to effectively perform this crucial function.

Another important consideration in the selection of the key man is his value in helping to overcome the pitfalls discussed previously in this chapter. As will be illustrated below, the key man is a critical resource for the specialist in avoiding or overcoming the pitfalls. If the key man is a functioning member of line management, he brings to the effort a useful source of leverage for guiding organization change.

The key man is the job enrichment specialist's contact with the client department. He should be high enough in the organization to prevent the specialist from being frozen out as problems arise and the normal tensions found in any organizational situation take effect. Ideally, he should function as a reference point for job enrichment, giving it direction within the context of the department. The key man should also be in a position to guarantee maintenance of the effort on a permanent basis after the specialist has left the scene. His position should be such that he is able to integrate the effort into future plans of the organization.

Those requirements suggest a middle-management person with full line responsibilities—an individual who grasps the value of the job enrichment concept and is willing to coordinate the effort for his department.

In most line organizations, it is possible to identify a position whose principal function is linking managers responsible for daily operations with upper management concerned with policy decisions. Region heads, division managers, directors, field supervisors, or the title immediately below such positions frequently serve such a function. Ideally, the key man role as developed here should be filled by an individual in a job serving this function.

Typically, such a key man will become well versed in job enrichment principles and will participate in training workshops and other crucial checkpoints of the effort, but will not be able to invest a large amount of time working closely with first-line supervisors. However, his position affords opportunities for integrating the effort into future plans of the department. Hopefully, his efforts are the inputs for turning the job enrichment process into a true exercise in structural organization development.

Two examples serve to illustrate the previous points. The first case involves a key man who was assigned to work with the job enrichment specialist on a full-time basis. This key man was a young administrator without much seniority within the client department. As the key man invested more time in the process, the line organization identified him more with job enrichment than with his own department. Eventually, he had less leverage in dealing with the department than the job enrichment specialist enjoyed.

Consequently, the key man was little help in dealing with internal departmental responses to the enrichment process, responses to which the job enrichment specialist was not privy. Occasionally, a front-line supervisor would become upset by an activity on the part of the specialist, but would not express his or her feelings to either the specialist or the key man. Rather, supervisors tended to internalize these incidents. At times, such incidents produced an underlying tension when line management met to discuss the project.

More serious were changes in operating procedures which, although conflicting with the intentions of job enrichment, were initiated by higher management and put into effect without discussion of the consequences for the job enrichment effort. This was not intentional; such incidents were the result of the fact that no one in the upper levels of the line organization was fully conversant with job enrichment principles.

Under such conditions, job enrichment developed an air

of being an ephemeral effort. Its character became that of something apart from and beyond the order of daily business. First-line supervisors perceived upper management was not expecting any significant changes in management style to be produced by the effort. Over time, the effort began losing momentum and the key man was not in a position to be influential in reversing the trend.

By way of contrast, the second case involves a situation where the key man was in a middle management slot with full line responsibilities. The changes which emerged out of the job enrichment effort were quite sweeping. Thus, many of the decisions raised questions in the corporate offices. It is difficult to overestimate the value of the key man in dealing with these issues. Himself an assistant vice president with line responsibilities, he served as a buffer in dealing with such problems as reassuring the corporate office that changes would be systematically introduced, getting approval to alter procedures, and reporting on the structural effects of the changes on the existing hierarchy of supervision.

The key man was also an asset in helping the specialist see that the supervisors did not "get in over their heads," that they had plans for acquiring the skills necessary to manage the redesigned jobs, and that proper control was established. Often, he provided first-line management with information regarding planned corporate changes which might affect their plans.

Further, the involvement of such an individual gave credibility to the job enrichment specialist's contention that the corporate office was prepared to allow them to make meaningful job changes. In contrast to the first example, first-line supervisors perceived the job enrichment effort as a long-range strategy with upper-management support.

Besides assuming responsibility for specific job enrichment efforts, the key man has another role: developing methods which help insure that job enrichment truly becomes part of the management strategy of the department and not the provincial knowledge of a few managers and supervisors. Here, the development of training programs for new managers emerges as useful and practical.

Incorporating employee utilization plans into yearly office business planning is another technique for building job enrichment into the department on a long-term basis. Requiring that new system proposals take into account job enrichment principles in the jobs they create is yet another. Once again, a key man with the characteristics previously described is in a position to take the steps necessary to see these activities become a reality in the department.

In summary, because job enrichment is an organization change process, the job enrichment specialist must be prepared to deal with the total organizational structure of a client department. The key man needs to be someone who can provide leverage in initiating and carrying through the change process. Of course, involvement of a key man with the characteristics outlined here does not guarantee successful resolution of the tensions and conflicts of organization change. However, it does provide for an individual whose position complements rather than duplicates that of the specialist and thus creates more flexibility on the part of those attempting to maintain the change process.

We have positioned the job enrichment specialist as an internal consultant. His role is that of a catalyst for change. In performing this role, he works closely with a key man, or coordinator, who is in a position within the client department to assist the specialist in guiding the change process over many of the difficulties inherent in organizational change. Thus, we have been discussing the proper leveraging of the job enrichment effort.

Of course, before an effort is leveraged, it must be determined where in the company job enrichment appears to be most feasible. This is the topic considered in Chapter 5.

5

selecting enrichable jobs

The first step in developing an enriched work structure within an organization is identification of those areas where job enrichment is particularly feasible. Properly applied, job enrichment has emerged as a valuable strategy of organization development. However, in addition to the widely reported success stories, there have been numerous efforts, not so widely reported, which have failed. Proper diagnostic work can greatly increase the probability of success and reduce the likelihood of becoming involved in an unsuccessful effort. An important part of the job enrichment specialist's role then is helping management identify areas of the company where job enrichment appears most feasible.

FOUR BASIC FEASIBILITY QUESTIONS

In attempting to determine whether job enrichment is feasible, an internal staff specialist needs to answer the following general questions:

1. Is it technically possible to change the job? Does enough flexibility exist in the present work structure to allow changes to be made?

2. Will employees respond favorably? Are there reasons to believe that employees will perceive an enriched job situation to be an improvement over the existing one?

3. What effect might job enrichment have on the work organization? What kinds of measurable results might be expected to occur as a result of a job enrichment effort?

4. Are there any general organization problems which are not job related, such as personnel policies, supervisory style, inadequate compensation, or inadequate training resources, and which are of such magnitude that implementing a job enrichment effort might be impeded?

Within any particular industry or company, the specific questions which might need to be considered under each of these broad questions may vary, but these four general questions summarize the basic issues with which the staff specialist must deal in determining the feasibility of job enrichment.

THREE CATEGORIES OF DATA

To the staff specialist attempting to answer these questions, three categories of data are available—symptomatic, attitudinal, and structural. Symptomatic data refers to measures of organizational performance which summarize overt employee behavior. Turnover, absenteeism, errors and other quality measures, poor productivity, and even reports on work slowdowns and sabotage are examples of this category of data.

By attitudinal data, we mean beliefs, opinions, and expectations expressed by employees and supervisors regarding the organization and their jobs within it.

Structural data refers to those aspects of the organization which are observable through patterns of work relationships. Superior–subordinate reporting relationships, work-flow patterns and the resulting employee interfaces, job content, and interdepartmental relationships and information flows are all dimensions of an organization structure.

Each of the three kinds of data provides insights into one or more of the four basic feasibility questions. However, because none of the data categories allows the specialist to deal with all of the questions, it is necessary to review all three sources of data in doing diagnostic work. Table 2 summarizes the relationship between the basic feasibility questions and categories of data. These relationships are considered in more detail in the following discussion.

Symptomatic Data

Symptomatic data, such as turnover rates, absenteeism figures, or rising customer complaints, are useful in two ways. First, they serve as red flags of emerging people-related problems. Second, should further investigation reveal the problems to be associated with job design, they give measures of costs currently being borne by the organization, improvement on which will benefit the company. Thus, symptomatic data provide at least a partial answer to one of our feasibility questions, "What are the possible effects?"

While symptomatic data can help identify problem areas within a work organization, it is important to remember that such indicators are symptomatic only; they do not specify what the underlying problems are, nor are they suggestive of particular solutions. Whether or not job redesign can be expected to be effective depends on the causes which underlie the symptom.

Another caution with regard to symptomatic data is remembering that symptoms which emerge in one job, or department, may be reflective of problems in another part of the organization. For example, in an insurance company, a clerical support unit for the underwriting department exhibited several symptoms often associated with poor job design, including lateness and absenteeism, poor service indices, and problems with papers being lost or misfiled. Research revealed low morale and job dissatisfaction among the clerks, and the initial impulse was to pursue ways of enriching their jobs.

However, an expanded diagnostic study revealed that if the work in the underwriting department were restructured, the basic clerical support unit could be eliminated. In addition, other benefits could be realized in underwriting through a restructuring of those jobs. The poor performance indicators in the clerical support unit were symptomatic of poor work organization in underwriting. Many times, diagnostic work reveals that a boring job can be eliminated through redesign of the other jobs in a department. In these instances, attempting to enrich the boring job is a misdirection of effort.

These illustrations demonstrate the problems in attempting to apply job enrichment in response to symptomatic data alone. Unusually negative symptomatic data serve as a warning that further investigation is necessary.

If further investigation reveals part of the problem to be associated with job design, an approximation of expected impact can be made. The term "approximation" is employed because models of organization dynamics with regard to human behavior are not precise enough to predict specific results and the specialist should avoid trying to do so.

This point is important because often managers will pressure a staff specialist for a specific target such as a 10 percent improvement in quality or a 12 percent increase in productivity or a 14 percent reduction in turnover, and so forth. When this happens, the specific number tends to become the sole objective of the effort, and our understanding of human behavior is nowhere near precise enough to allow the specialist to make such a projection. Based upon his diagnostic work, the specialist may feel comfortable stating, "I believe quality will improve as a result of more clearly defined work" and giving his reasons for making such a statement. But he should avoid getting locked into a short-term objective which (1) he cannot be sure of meeting and (2) causes managers to buy in for the wrong reasons.

Of course, quality, absenteeism, productivity, and whatever other indices are important to management should be measured, so that job enrichment's impact on the organization can be assessed. The point is that the specialist should avoid getting locked into a situation in which management is looking for a very specific short-term result which he is in no way certain

Table 2. Relationship between basic study questions and input from different kinds of data.

	SYMPTOMATIC DATA	ATTITUDINAL DATA	STRUCTURAL DATA
Is job enrichment technically possible?			**High Input** Can identify the basic opportunities for enrichment changes. Also help in assessing what layout and equipment changes would be necessary.
How will employees react?		**High Input** Can identify current employee awareness of job characteristics. If job awareness is low, a positive impact on employee interest is possible.	

| What are the possible effects? | **High Input** Can give a measure of the magnitude of existing problems which might be expected to be alleviated by job changes. | **Moderate Input** May identify specific work-related problems which, if changed, will result in improvements. If interviews reveal a concern over lack of learning opportunities, or knowing how well they are doing or sense of ownership, job enrichment should be effective. |
| Are there other conditions of importance? | | **High Input** Can identify dominant employee concerns which can be followed up on. May reveal more job related factors which are important. Interviews with supervisors can provide a measure of their receptivity to change. |

he can achieve. Buying into such a situation does not leverage the strategy of managing through job design very securely in the company over the long run.

Attitudinal Data

Attitudinal data obtained from personal interviews and formal questionnaires are especially valuable inasmuch as they relate to three of the feasibility questions: (1) How will employees react? (2) What are the possible effects? (3) Are there other organization conditions of importance?

Employees' responses to interview questions regarding their feelings toward their jobs can provide an insight into how they might respond to job enrichment changes. If, for example, the response to the question "How do you get your work?" is "My supervisor just gives us our work in batches" or "It is just assigned" or "When we're not busy, we get more from the supervisor," further probing is appropriate. These responses are often clues to a low degree of concern for the job because "It just passes through." Therefore, changes which build client identification should be received favorably.

The same is true for responses to the question "Who depends upon you to do a good job?" Answers such as "I don't know," "The company," or "My supervisor" are indications that identification with a real client would add an important element of responsibility to the job.

If the question "How do you know if you are doing a good job?" elicits a response such as "If I don't get yelled at," "I don't know," or "One of the problems around here is that you really don't have any idea," it is perhaps indicative of a lack of feedback. Since most people want to know how well they are performing, most employees react favorably to improved feedback systems.

Open-ended interviews often produce insights into work-related problems such as poor communications, bottlenecks, or having to do things twice. If providing a more complete piece of work can eliminate these, the specialist has additional information on how job design might affect the performance of the organization.

Should the interviews reveal widespread concern over lack of opportunities to learn new skills, lack of a sense of ownership of the work, or lack of information on performance, job enrichment should increase employee interest in the work. In labor-intensive organizations, this increased interest can be expected to translate into improved performance.

Finally, interviews and questionnaires often reveal employee concerns which are not related to job content but are important and should be dealt with. An overly autocratic supervisor, for example, may be causing turnover problems. Identification of these types of problems is important because they should be dealt with directly and because their existence would impede any job redesign effort.

Structural Data

Structural data provide information regarding opportunities for enriching a specific set of jobs. Thus, they relate to the first feasibility question. A given job may be boring and difficult to fill, but if no opportunities for enriching the job exist, then job enrichment cannot be considered a viable strategy.

In attempting to determine structural opportunities for job enrichment, the job enrichment specialist is attempting to determine the possibilities for assigning work on a user basis or for task combination or for building more decision making and control into the job or for providing better feedback.

Structural indicators of enrichment potential [1] which should be investigated further include:

1. *Functions performed twice.* Are there operations performed at one point in a given flow and then done again by someone else in the same flow? If so, these may indicate incomplete jobs.

2. *Dual reporting relationships.* The existence of these may result in lack of clarity concerning tasks to be done, or in decision making being taken out of the individual's hands.

3. *Multiple authority limits.* Are there several levels of authority among employees, without significant variation in the complexity of exercising authority throughout those levels? Often this indicator exists where management is trying to create an artificial "career ladder."

4. *Similar job titles.* Are there several title layers for the same basic job—for example, claim clerk, senior claim clerk, chief claim clerk? Once again, this indicator can reflect attempts at creating career ladders.

5. *Excessive job titles.* A high proportion of job titles to actual number of employees may reflect an excessively fragmented work flow.

6. *Special checking or reviewing functions.* The existence of job titles including the words "checker" or "reviewer" or "control" may reflect fragmented responsibility for work quality. This means that responsibility for doing the job and responsibility for determining whether the job has been done right are located in two different positions.

7. *Pools (typing pools, maintenance pools, and the like).* Usually, pools result in fragmented, incomplete jobs from which little feedback is received.

8. *Special communication units.* The existence of these units usually means that client contact has been removed from basic operations-type jobs.

9. *Troubleshooting jobs.* Job titles such as "expediter," "coordinator," and the like, usually mean operations people are not involved in problem-solving activities. The troubleshooters have the top half of the jobs of others.

10. *Several people on one machine.* Where more than one person performs jobs on the same unit of machinery, incomplete pieces of work may result.

11. *Product pooling.* When a product from one department is pooled before going to the next department, operators usually have little responsibility for the problems confronting the operators in that next department. No client identification exists.

12. *Crisscrossing job layouts.* This consists of job layouts where interdependent job performers do not relate as teams but

in a random fashion. A crisscrossing job layout occurs, for example, when a machine operator's job assignment includes several machines serviced by different maintenance people (see Exhibit 6).

Sometimes very sound technical reasoning underlies the existence of these structural conditions, and they cannot be changed. Often, however, changes can be made. For example, in the case of multiple authority limits, are the limits based upon documented skill differentials which additional training cannot easily overcome (approving a business loan requires different knowledge from approving a small personal loan)? Or are they based only upon time in grade (the procedure for approving a $50 check is the same as the procedure for approving a $1,000 check)? Often the distinction is how long you have been with the company.

In analyzing structural data, the specialist should also consider existing layout and equipment design. Sometimes it is

Exhibit 6. A crisscrossing job layout.

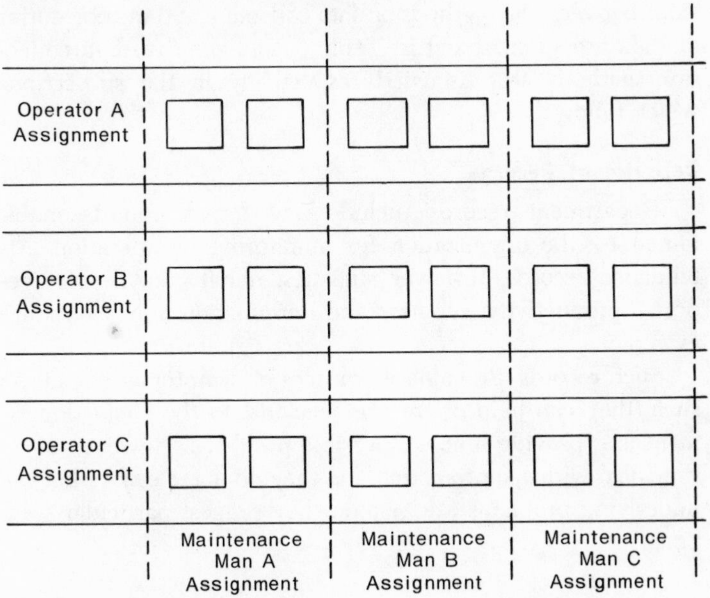

possible to get the job done differently, but to do so would require layout and equipment changes which are just too expensive. In these cases, the specialist cannot suggest job enrichment in the present situation. He can, however, keep his findings in mind pending the start-up of a new plant or office operations where these problems won't have him locked in.

FIVE METHODS OF DATA COLLECTION

We have seen that in order to answer the basic feasibility questions, the specialist needs to consider three categories of data. Five basic data collection techniques are available to the job enrichment specialist for tapping the categories of data: (1) department records, (2) questionnaires, (3) interviews, (4) direct observation, and (5) charting.

Each of the five data collection techniques taps one or more of the categories of data. As each source of data presents a different aspect of the situation, the specialist cannot rely solely upon any one method of data collection. The relationships between the methods of data collection and the categories of data are summarized in Table 3, and the five data collection methods are discussed respectively in the subsections which follow.

Department Records

Department records include any formal reports maintained by the organization for monitoring its operation. Attendance records, turnover statistics, quality and service reports, productivity reports, and termination interviews are examples.

Such records are valuable sources of symptomatic data. As such, they can help orient the specialist to the client department and provide hints of possible problems. However, since they deal with symptomatic data, they do not specify what the underlying problems are, nor do they suggest particular solutions.

Occasionally, department records can be a source of attitude data. Termination interviews, for example, if well done, might provide clues to employee attitudes toward their jobs. However, in most companies, such interviews are not intensively and carefully conducted, and the specialist should not rely on them very heavily.

Also, staffing reports can provide clues to how a work unit is structured. Job descriptions are another type of record useful in this regard. However, care must be taken to verify data obtained from these records as they may not accurately reflect what actually happens on the job.

Questionnaires

As diagnostic tools, well-designed formal questionnaires with established validity and reliability standards are sensitive measures of employee attitudes toward their work. Some good questionnaires which are applicable in many industrial and commercial situations are available, but many companies prefer to develop one specifically for their own use.

Questionnaires highlight employee perceptions of the work situation. These perceptions are often the first step in coming to an understanding of the conditions which underlie symptomatic data.

Questionnaires also give the specialist a reliable measure of current employee attitudes which indicate how much room for improvement exists and, more specifically, where some of the most important improvement opportunities are to be found. If the instrument measures both job content dimensions and environmental factors, important environmental factors which could inhibit implementation of job enrichment may be discovered.

However, it is important for the specialist to remember that formal questionnaires produce statistical distributions. As with symptomatic data, more than one set of conditions of causal factors often influences the distribution. Therefore, additional investigation is necessary.

Table 3. Relationship between data collection techniques and sources of data.

	SYMPTOMATIC SOURCE	ATTITUDINAL SOURCE	STRUCTURAL SOURCE
Records	**High Relationship** Can help identify specific problem areas within the work organization.	**Moderate Relationship** Certain types of records, such as exit interviews, sometimes provide information on attitudes.	**Moderate Relationship** Staffing reports and charts can provide clues to the way a work unit is structured.
Questionnaires	**Moderate Relationship** For example, can demonstrate a general morale problem.	**High Relationship** Well-designed questionnaires are the most sensitive measures of attitudes.	**Low Relationship** Some questionnaires can indicate weak aspect of job structure. Usually inferences must be made.

Interviews	**Low Relationship** Such interviews can occasionally produce evidence of a symptomatic problem not previously identified. Usually few surprises here.	**High Relationship** Detailed unstructured interviews provide a rich data base on employee attitudes toward their jobs.	**Moderate Relationship** Often the interview can elicit factual information on structural characteristics of the work organization.
Direct Observation		**Moderate Relationship** Occasionally, the specialist will observe expressions of employee attitudes toward the job. This almost always involves inference making by the specialist.	**High Relationship** The specialist can directly observe significant structural characteristics of the organization.
Charting			**High Relationship** An extension of direct observation, well-prepared charts clearly illustrate the structural character of the organization.

Interviews

Properly conducted, the semistructured interview can provide both detailed attitudinal data and, from some employees, concrete information regarding jobs and other structural data. Building on a basic set of questions, the interview should be a conversation between the specialist and employee, during which the specialist explores the topics of concern that naturally emerge from the employee's responses.

Standard interview techniques for getting the employee to talk freely—such as open-ended questions expressing interest and understanding, restatement, and silence—can be used to generate data. Here is a sampling of basic questions along with typical clues they generate.

Basic Questions	Some Possible Responses	What Can Be Learned through Follow-up Questioning
1. Describe how you typically spend your day.	Description of work activity.	Basic tasks; how work is assigned; what things go wrong; relationship to others.
2. How do you get your work?	"My supervisor gives us all batches." "It is just assigned." "When not busy, we get more."	Perception of client identification and product identification. Also, structural basis of work assignments.
3. Who depends on you to do a good job?	"I don't know." "The company." "My supervisor." "Another worker."	Perception of client relationship, if any.
4. How do you know if you are doing a good job?	"If I don't get yelled at." "I don't know." "If the books balance."	Perception of feedback, if any.
5. What happens if you make a mistake?	"I get yelled at." "The foreman takes care of it." "I don't know."	Perception of feedback. Also, involvement in problem solving; relationship to supervisor.
6. What do you like least (best) about working here?	Comment on dislikes (likes).	Employee perceptions of problems, strengths, and weaknesses of the organization. Those things that are foremost on their minds.

Basic Questions	Some Possible Responses	What Can Be Learned through Follow-up Questioning
7. Remember when you were being trained? What might have been done differently to help you?	"They need to spend a little more time; some trainers get disgusted too quickly." "The trainers don't have the time to spend." "My supervisor also showed me a different way."	Employee perception of training effort.

The emergence method of interviewing, described by John Drake, is particularly useful in job enrichment diagnostic studies.[2] In this approach, emphasis is placed upon understanding the unique situation rather than seeking a preconceived set of organizational characteristics. While Drake writes primarily about assessment interviewing, the techniques and methods he describes are valid for data collection interviewing as well.

Using the emergence method, the job enrichment specialist attempts to understand how the organization in question functions with regard to its employees—how it solves problems, how it tries to motivate, and how it utilizes workers' aptitudes and skills. In short, through the eyes of employees, the specialist develops a mental portrait of the organization that he can relate to the data he collected through other methods and can then apply to the problem in question.

In completing his portrait, the specialist develops hypotheses which he pursues in the interview through additional questions. Substantiated hypotheses are then further pursued for verification with other employees.

Direct Observation

Direct observation of the work unit in question is the most effective source of structural data. Watching the work performed by supervisors and employees provides a good feel for the opportunities to change jobs.

In general, while observing a work unit, the specialist wants to determine (1) how closely the existing jobs approximate enriched jobs, (2) how much flexibility for changing jobs appears to exist, and (3) what equipment and work-flow changes would be necessary.

For example, the specialist may observe supervisors heavily involved in production work (particularly the more complicated items) which could be spread out to the employees below them, or he may see several workers performing fragmented jobs on the same piece of machinery. Each is an indication of incomplete jobs which, with some alteration in work load assignments, might be made more complete. Upon observing these situations, the specialist would want to explore the possibilities further.

Charting

At times an operation is so complex that the job enrichment specialist feels he needs more systematic evidence regarding the structural conditions in the client department. In these instances, he can utilize the standard charting procedures developed by engineering and work simplification people. Flow charts, work distribution charts, and organization charts are usually useful in these situations.[3] Charting is an extension of direct observation, and the data are employed for the same purpose.

INTERPRETING THE DATA

The five data collection techniques enable the specialist to move systematically from symptomatic data to attitudinal data to structural data. Collecting all three categories of data enables the specialist to address the four basic feasibility questions.

Conclusions drawn from a diagnostic study always involve interpretive judgments on the part of the job enrichment specialist. To interpret data reliably, the specialist is dependent upon the theoretical models that guide his thinking.

More generally, the crucial role of models in all forms of

diagnostic work should be recognized. Absence of any model will result in the pursuit of unrelated tangents with little consistency. Further, since all data require interpretation, lack of a specified model means the substitution of unspecified bias on the part of the researcher. Explicit models allow the specialist to test his assumptions and learn from experience.

The models being suggested here are the three-part model of an enriched job presented in Chapter 3 and a change model which believes structural change produces changes in employee performance and attitudes (as discussed in Chapter 1). Among the assumptions underlying these models of work design is the belief that most people do respond positively to work experiences which provide opportunities for recognition, responsibility, achievement, and growth, and that task achievement leads to increased motivation and is a strong instrument for inducing behavior change.

The specialist must be convinced of the validity of these assumptions because rarely will he encounter data in the diagnostic study that will specifically indicate job redesign will have this effect. Rather, data must be evaluated in light of the models.

The data collection and interpretation process can be illustrated by a diagnostic study performed in a clerical operation in the field office of an insurance company. The clerical unit processed payments and benefits on various kinds of insurance policies. Since most of the records were stored in a computer in the home office, much of the clerical work involved preparing data input for entry into the real-time system. Management was interested in identifying areas in which to introduce job enrichment, and this unit was one of the areas selected for diagnostic work.

Records maintained by the data processing department indicated no major symptoms, although turnover was slightly higher in these jobs than in other field offices. Production and quality figures were acceptable, although room for improvement existed. In short, it was a statistically average department.

Direct observation revealed the jobs were fragmented. Each clerk was doing only one or two of the different types of clerical work being performed in the unit. Work was distributed on a batch basis, each clerk receiving a set number of items each day. Supervisors did all correspondence and dealt with all problems from agents or policyholders.

Interviews indicated that clerks did not particularly dislike working in the clerical unit although several expressed a desire to learn more about different types of work in the unit. Comments like "I think it would be better if you could learn more types of operations" or "Two years of doing the same thing can get a little tiresome" were not uncommon. Only a few girls had an accurate idea of where their work went. None knew what kind of correspondence came in from the field.

A questionnaire designed to measure aspects of employee satisfaction with both working conditions (such as office space, supervision, compensation, and equipment) and the job itself (interest, responsibility, authority to perform the job well, and so forth) was administered. The results indicated satisfaction with working conditions to be consistent with or, in some cases, better than company norms. But satisfaction with the job itself was one standard deviation below company norms.

When the data were matched with our four feasibility questions, this clerical operation appeared to be a good candidate for job enrichment. With regard to question 1 (Is it technically possible to change the job?), the answer was yes. The observations revealed opportunities for task combination and reassigning work on an agency, rather than batch, basis. This change would make the job correspond more closely to the first part of the model of an enriched job.

Further, opportunities were also present for getting clerks involved in correspondence with agents and policyholders, which would help them with service problems. Job design changes in these areas would affect the second and third parts of the model of an enriched job.

The second feasibility question relates to employee response to the changes. Are there reasons to believe that employees will perceive an enriched job situation to be an improvement over the existing one? Again, the answer was yes. Employee comments expressing a willingness to learn more about the work they were doing indicated a positive response from employees. Also, the questionnaire indicated no major dissatisfactions with working conditions and more than average disinterest in the work itself. This data tended to suggest that most employees in the unit would respond favorably to changes in their jobs.

Since neither the interviews nor the questionnaire data revealed high dissatisfaction with any particular aspect of the work environment, it also appeared that the answer to the fourth feasibility question (Are there any general organization problems which are not job related which are of such magnitude as to impede implementation of job enrichment?) was no. That left only the third question (What effect might job enrichment have on the work organization?) to be answered.

As was discussed earlier in this chapter, because our models of human behavior do not consist of perfect relationships, it is difficult to predict exactly what the effect on an organization might be. In this particular instance, the kinds of changes which appeared to be possible in the work structure, coupled with the attitudinal responses obtained through interviews and the questionnaire, led to a prediction of improved job satisfaction among the employees.

This prediction was based on the fact that people usually respond favorably to more complete jobs, over which they have more control. And the attitudinal data indicated considerable room for improvement. As a result of improved interest in the work, it was felt that turnover would improve relative to other departments. This prediction was based upon the fact that no other major factor seemed to be causing a disproportionate amount of turnover.

Upon examination of the kinds of problems which agents and policyholders frequently experienced in getting transactions processed, it also appeared that combining certain tasks and giving the clerks direct contact with the agents and policy-holders would result in improved quality. Similar kinds of changes in other companies had resulted in improved quality without a loss in productivity.

Since management was particularly concerned about the employees' lack of interest in their jobs, believing that over the course of several years this situation would hurt the company, it was agreed upon that improved interest in the work as measured by the questionnaire would be the principal objective.

Further, quality would be carefully tracked, as improvements here would improve the company's competitive position among the independent agents in the marketplace. Thus, improvement in quality of work being performed was also to be a measure of the success of the effort. In addition, of course, management would continue to monitor all of the traditional measures of unit performance.

The previous case illustrates the way in which inferences must be drawn from data. Conclusions must be based not only on the present situation, but on anticipated effects of changes in the work situation. For example, skeptical supervisors often become more enthusiastic after seeing the impact which one or two changes have on employees; or apathetic employees often become more interested when actually doing different things, solving problems, and receiving positive feedback. While these are not perfectly predictable outcomes, experience indicates the probabilities are on the side of enriched job design.

MANAGEMENT'S WILLINGNESS TO CHANGE

Performance of the diagnostic study is an important part of the job enrichment process. Good diagnostic work can significantly reduce the likelihood of initiating an unsuccessful job enrichment effort. If the conclusion of the diagnostic study is a viable strategy for job enrichment, two important points need to be made to management:

First, management must understand that implementing job enrichment is a process of management development. (This point will be discussed in detail in Chapter 7.) Enriched jobs cannot be engineered because supervisory behavior affects the job content of subordinates, especially with regard to the second dimension of our model of an enriched job—the amount of control a subordinate has over his work. For job enrichment to work, a strong supervisory organization must be developed as a spinoff of the implementation process. The burden of devising job changes and implementing them must rest with managers and supervisors. Thus, management must be prepared to be patient with supervisors and be willing to tolerate some mistakes.

Second, management must be prepared to allow some significant changes to take place. It is, of course, rare for management to consider everything open to change. And it will express the desire to take a hard look at any major change proposals. Too easy a sale at the diagnostic stage might indicate management does not realize the full implications of the job enrichment concept. What needs to be determined is whether the restrictions which management may place on the job enrichment effort preclude changes of the magnitude necessary for success. And, is management willing to try changes in the area of job design and learn from the results?

This is a qualitative decision on the part of the job enrichment specialist. One way to determine the answer is to explicitly discuss the kinds of changes which might have to occur. In so doing, the specialist is helping management understand more clearly the nature of the strategy on which it is about to embark.

After the selection of an area in which to implement job enrichment, the next major task is redesigning the jobs so that they more closely resemble our model of an enriched job. Accomplishing this is the topic of Chapter 6.

REFERENCES

1. David A. Whitsett is responsible for developing several of these clues. See Whitsett, "Where Are Your Unenriched Jobs?" *Harvard Business Review,* January–February 1975.

2. John D. Drake, *Interviewing for Managers* (New York: American Management Associations, 1972).

3. A good discussion on these charts can be found in *Auditing for System Improvement* (Cleveland: Association for System Management, 1972).

6

a systems approach
to redesigning jobs

Once it has been determined that the jobs in a particular unit or department are enrichable, the task becomes redesigning them so that they more closely correspond to our model of an enriched job. Redesigning jobs, as we have discussed in earlier chapters, involves organization change.

One must be as concerned about the method through which the jobs are redesigned as about the projected job characteristics themselves, for if the design process is not handled properly, managers and supervisors are unlikely to be committed to enriched job design and eventual failure will be predictable. Experience has demonstrated that the process of redesigning jobs is crucial to the eventual success of a job enrichment effort. Elements of the redesign process which are important to success include:

1. Working with the proper "vertical slice" of the organization.
2. Content of the job redesign workshop.
3. Building completeness into jobs.
4. Identifying the decisions over which job holders will exercise control.
5. Designing feedback systems into the jobs.

Each of those elements will be discussed in turn in the following sections.

WORKING WITH THE PROPER "VERTICAL SLICE" OF THE ORGANIZATION

A basic principle which must underlie the redesign process is that it be an exercise in management development. The appropriate role of the job enrichment specialist is that of a catalyst, helping managers and supervisors understand why enriched job design works and how to approach redesign of the jobs they supervise, suggesting ways of overcoming problems, and helping them devise strategies for selling their ideas to management.

In short, the job enrichment specialist is a professional resource. He should not undertake to redesign the jobs himself or assume the role of the expert telling managers what will be done. His approach to managers and supervisors should be built on a human resources rather than a human relations model [1]—that is, the approach should utilize the abilities of the managers and supervisors rather than allow them to comment on and, in some instances, modify the ideas of the specialist.

Management development occurs when a manager accomplishes an important goal through the use of a new approach or technique.[2] Achievement as a result of a concentrated effort in the application of new skills reinforces the validity of those skills for solving managerial problems and increases the probability that the manager will apply the skills in the future. It is a basic task of the job enrichment specialist to structure a concentrated effort in the application of job enrichment principles which results in an achieving experience for the managers and supervisors involved.

By the nature of the concept, implementing job enrichment requires the support of several layers of management. First, line supervision cannot implement a concentrated job enrichment effort if managers at higher levels are insisting on more direct organization controls. Earlier chapters emphasized the necessity of understanding and support at the executive level of management. Equally important is cooperation among the various levels of managers with daily operational responsibilities in the organization, that is, those managers and supervisors who are directly responsible for the day-to-day operation of specific facilities.

This responsibility typically encompasses several layers of managers who regularly interact with each other. For example, in manufacturing the operation level of management might include the following positions: plant manager, assistant plant manager, superintendent, general foreman, and foreman. In the office situation, their counterparts might be office manager, department manager, assistant manager, and supervisor. If job enrichment is going to be successful in any given plant or office, individuals at each level need to be involved in the redesign process. Indeed, they are going to have to function as a team, with each level knowing it has the support of the one above it.

Starting with the first level of supervision over the jobs to be redesigned and working up through the chain of command to the principal manager over the operation in question on a daily basis, one can identify a team of managers which for convenience sake can be referred to as a "vertical slice" of the organization. This vertical slice is the management team which the job enrichment specialist and the key man need to work with in redesigning jobs (see Chapter 4). As a group, this vertical slice will participate in a job redesign workshop, the content of which will be discussed in the next section.

Identification of the vertical slice is a critical activity but one which is easy to perform. Every member of supervision, from the first-line supervisor over the jobs in question to the manager who is clearly identified with day-to-day operations, should be involved. Usually, this includes three to five levels of managers, ranging from foreman or supervisors to plant or office manager. This maintains the political integrity of the management chain and insures that everyone who shares in the basic responsibility for performance of the given unit is involved in the redesign process.

Two common mistakes which can seriously affect the outcome of a job enrichment effort are not taking the vertical slice high enough or low enough. Under no circumstances should the job enrichment specialist and key man allow themselves to be talked out of the participation of a manager who is clearly influential in the managing of the shop or office. Accepting at face value the statement "Look, I understand what you are doing and I think it's great, but you don't need me there" almost guarantees future problems.

Such a statement indicates that the manager either lacks the commitment necessary to help the effort succeed, doesn't really understand what is going to be done (few managers are about to let their supervisors make significant changes in jobs without their own input), or both. The manager needs to hear everything which is said at the workshop and to make sure that the plans formulated take into account any constraints he may be concerned about.

Likewise, no first-line supervisor should be left to "cover the store while we are gone." Experienced workers and supervisors from other areas can cover the store. All supervisors who are expected to implement job enrichment changes need to participate in the redesign process.

CONTENT OF THE JOB REDESIGN WORKSHOP

After the proper vertical slice has been identified, the next step is conducting an intensive three- or four-day workshop, the purpose of which is the basic redesign of jobs. Training in job enrichment principles per se should be held to the minimum necessary to begin the redesign process. This reasoning is based on our previous discussion on management development. True development occurs through specific accomplishments. Many opportunities for discussing job enrichment techniques will occur during the redesign process itself.

The workshop should be held at a location removed from

the immediate work area. Many times a management training center is available or a local hotel facility. Whether the workshop lasts three or four days depends upon the time available. However, whatever does not get accomplished at the workshop must be finished through committee and individual efforts. Since the workshop setting represents an opportunity for uninterrupted thinking, and a momentum builds up over the first couple of days, a four-day session usually results in significantly more work being accomplished over a shorter time period.

The specific content of any workshop must, of course, be adjusted to reflect the particular group which is participating in the session. How much training time will be required, how difficult the redesign process will be, and how much time will be required to accomplish these tasks depend among other things on the level of sophistication of the group, on how well they already work together as a team, and on the complexity of the work flow for which the jobs are being redesigned.

Creating a workshop design specifically for the needs of a particular group requires skills in group development work on the part of the job enrichment specialist. Whatever the design of the workshop, three tasks which must be accomplished are (1) the design of complete jobs, (2) determination of the amount of control the job incumbent will be permitted to exercise over his job, and (3) design of feedback systems for the job. Techniques for accomplishing these tasks are the topics for the remainder of this chapter.

BUILDING THE BASIC JOB

A basic approach to the redesign of jobs which emerged out of Robert Ford's initial Bell System studies has been *brainstorming*.[3] Simply defined, brainstorming is an unrestrained exchange of ideas among a group of people. All ideas are listed, without concern for practicality, for later consideration. The basic advantage of brainstorming is that it creates an atmosphere in which people look at a problem in new ways and build on each other's ideas. Often it sows the seeds of innovative courses of action which might not otherwise be considered.

Using the brainstorming technique, members of the group randomly suggest changes which they believe will enrich the job. No ground rules exist except that no member of the group can criticize an idea by another member during the brainstorming process and even contradictory suggestions are added to the list. The basic objective is to get as many ideas out in the open as possible. An underlying dynamic is that often the idea of one individual triggers a different suggestion in the mind of another. The result is a synergistic buildup within the group, with individuals building on the suggestions of others.

After the list is completed, the group reviews it, first to identify those items which truly change the job itself and then a second time to consider the advantages and disadvantages associated with each item which has been identified in the first review. Finally, a set of items is selected for implementation.

The brainstorming approach has proven effective as a method for redesigning jobs.[4] A major advantage of brainstorming is its capacity for getting the participants involved, for tapping ideas which might otherwise remain undiscussed, and for establishing a freewheeling atmosphere of give and take which is conducive to planning for change.

As with any technique, however, brainstorming has associated disadvantages as well. In particular, it has a tendency to result in a piecemeal approach to the redesign of jobs; taking individual ideas on different jobs in a work unit and putting them together in an attempt to enrich as many jobs as possible.

The emphasis in such an approach tends toward reform rather than complete redesign. A consequence of this emphasis is that opportunities for reorganization of the entire work unit so that the unit might better accomplish its basic objectives are often missed, or not recognized until considerable time and effort have been invested in "reforming" the structure of individual jobs. Perhaps certain jobs need not exist at all.

Perhaps a more basic change in the way work is organized would eliminate certain ineconomies which have occurred as a result of the basic method through which the jobs were originally designed. These possibilities are the kind which are often raised by individuals trained in the system approach to organization processes.

In response to these issues, which are valid ones, and a general feeling that the basic job (the first part of our model of an enriched job) should not be "up for grabs," an alternative technology for redesigning jobs has evolved.[5] It is based on the assumption that a more wholistic approach to the design problem will result in a system of jobs best suited to the particular demands and constraints of the work unit in question.

The first step of the new technology is designing the first part of our definition of an enriched job; the completeness of individual jobs. This process requires identification of three basic elements: the mission of the work unit, the primary clients of the work unit for whom that mission is performed, and the tasks which have to get done if the mission is to be successfully completed.

The Mission of the Work Unit

Mission, in the sense we are using it here, corresponds to what in system analysis is often called the function of the system. What, specifically, is the work unit in question supposed to do? The group should be asked to specifically state what they believe to be the mission of the work unit. This will often produce a wide variety of statements of varying degrees of sophistication. For example, managers in an underwriting unit of an insurance company stated that the mission was:

—Providing fast and accurate service to policyholders.
—Processing new policy coverage and renewal and changes in policy coverage.
—Providing field support for agents.
—Deciding which risks should be covered by the company.

The job enrichment specialist must get the group to think in terms of what service or services does the unit perform which is both unique and crucial to the functioning of the enterprise. What is the "piece" which the unit contributes to all the other pieces in the production process which allows the organization to continue to function. In the case of the underwriting unit, the group rewrote the mission to read, "Get on the books that part of the business which is made available to us through our agents in a manner which involves proper pricing and balanced expenses, and on a basis which allows the agent to remain competitive."

Further discussion resulted in agreement that "Allowing the agent to remain competitive involved taking into consideration the total business package available to the company and providing the agent with fast, accurate service." Thus, the basic contribution of the underwriting unit was "Managing the business produced by the agency force." This was the basic mission of the underwriting unit.

Afterward, there was agreement as to the dimensions involved in managing the business, such as volume, loss ratios, service times, and the like. These were added to the statement of mission.

With a specific statement of mission agreed on by the group, it then becomes possible to measure the way work is organized in the unit against the criteria of whether or not it contributes to accomplishment of the mission. The first step of this process is determination of the primary client.

The Primary Client

In this step, agreement is obtained on who is the primary client, or receiver, for whom the mission is performed. As managers will readily admit, almost all work units experience competing demands for different kinds of services from elements outside their boundaries. This is especially true of administrative type work units.

For example, an underwriting unit in the field office of a casualty-property insurance company experiences demands from insureds for policy information, from agents for new policies and other services, from the home office for certain records and transactions, and from the claim department for information regarding policy coverage of insureds making claims. The unfortunate result often is a policy of responding to whatever pressures are the greatest at the moment.

In identifying the primary client, managers and supervisors are being asked to select, from among those various elements that are placing demands upon their unit, that element which should receive first priority if their basic mission is to be accomplished. Once the primary client has been identified, individual jobs will be organized around the client situation, with procedures for satisfying the demands of other elements built into the jobs so that meeting these demands does not sacrifice accomplishment of the work unit's mission.

To determine the primary client, the first procedure is to ask the group to list all the different groups or elements which place demands upon the work unit for output. Usually a list of four to eight elements will be produced. In preparing the list, categories of elements should be used. For example, in a key punch department, the category "user departments" is sufficient rather than listing all the departments. Or, in an underwriting department, "agents" should be used rather than listing all the agencies serviced by the unit.

Individuals from a given level of the vertical slice often perceive different elements than those at other levels, so just producing the list can prove educational. Having produced the list, the workshop leader should ask the group the question, "Given the mission which we have just identified, which element on the list should be our primary client?"

Depending upon the work unit being analyzed, the answer to that question may either be obvious or involve considerable debate. For example, to continue with our underwriting unit, it is often unclear initially to the participants whether the insured or the agent is the primary client. The job enrichment specialist and key man should encourage this discussion, emphasizing that the primary client should be the one with whom the unit has most frequent, direct contact over a wide range of problems in striving to satisfy its mission.

When agreement has been reached on the primary client, the basis for one dimension of a complete piece of work has been identified.

The Tasks of the Work Unit

With the client identified, the next problem before the group is a listing of all the tasks which are performed in the work unit while it is attempting to complete its mission. If charting was performed during the diagnostic study, considerable time can be saved by distributing to the group the task lists completed then. The group can then question, delete from, or add to the list.

If charting was not performed, the group will have to list all the tasks in the workshop. Examples of tasks are "reviewing the application for completion," "computing billing rates," "setting up the machines," and so forth. The task listing needs to be complete as it is the basis for the second dimension of a complete piece of work.

Building the Jobs

When agreement on both the primary client and the task listing has been obtained, the question should be put before the group, "Is there any way one individual can perform all these tasks for a group of clients?" In other words, the question is whether or not work assignments could be made on a client basis, with an individual's job being to provide the full range of services to his or her clients.

The group should be left alone to consider this problem. In discussing the assignment, the only guidelines are (1) forget about existing job titles and proceed as though designing an entirely new structure, and (2) forget about current employee performance.

After a period of time, the group will usually decide that such an arrangement is unrealistic. The job enrichment specialist and key man should review with the group the reasons for this conclusion, helping them to overcome any problems which might, with further discussion, be overcome. Most likely, however, valid reasons regarding the unfeasibility of such an arrangement will exist. For example, often the range of tasks is so large as to require fundamentally different sets of skills; or clear conflicts in timing, such as two different tasks having to be performed concurrently, may exist.

In this situation, the group should be reminded of what a complete job that would have been were it possible to design it. The group should then be asked whether or not the tasks could be structured and work assigned in such a way that two individuals could serve a given set of clients, with a clear division of labor in terms of tasks existing between the two individuals. The group should be left alone to again consider this possibility.

This cycle of events should be repeated until the group arrives at a set of jobs which match as closely as possible the first part of the model of an enriched job. The result should be a set of work assignments based upon clients rather than function, with each individual responsible for a specific set of tasks for his clients. In designing the new job, the discussions between group members, the job enrichment specialist, and the key man provide a unique opportunity for supervision to consider the range of possibilities and problems in the structuring of work.

It is important that the jobs which are designed through this process be considered as starting points, subject to change on the basis of experience. This design will be open to modification during implementation of the changes.

IDENTIFYING THE DECISIONS OVER WHICH JOB HOLDERS WILL EXERCISE CONTROL

The second part of the model of an enriched job deals with the amount of discretion the individual exercises in performing his or her job. No matter how complete the job is, if the incumbent has no say over how the job is to be performed, the experience is not very enriching.

At this point the group should brainstorm the discretionary aspect of each of the new jobs. The question before the group should be, "Given the above job, what decisions, adjustments, exceptions, and the like, are going to need to be made in performing the job?" The only ground rule is that no one attack someone else's ideas during the brainstorming. At the moment, what is needed is a complete list—the next step will be to determine whether each item should be exercised by employees or supervision. During the brainstorming session, a free exchange of ideas is to occur. Such a list should be prepared for each job which has been designed.

Once the brainstorming has been completed, the group then evaluates each idea on the list, arriving at a final list of decision items identified respectively as to whether they are to be part of the job or the responsibility of others (specialists, supervisors, and the like). Usually, this requires considerable discussion. Many ideas may be left on the list with the understanding they will be discussed further. Some of the ideas may require management approval.

In discussing the brainstorm list, the group should be reminded that not every employee needs to be permitted to exercise a given decision. Implementation will be selective. What is desired is a basic list of decisions on which there is agreement among the group that (1) the decision should really be part of the job and (2) at least some of the unit's people are capable of making that decision.

An example of a decision which frequently appears on brainstorm lists is, "Allow employees to set own work priorities." This suggestion is usually intended to allow the job incumbent to schedule his production runs, or in clerical operations, to determine which case to deal with first.

A frequent counterargument to this proposal is, "But we have certain deadlines to meet." Another counterargument is, "In setting priorities, we know what other jobs may be coming in." The questions which must be asked of both these arguments are, "What would happen if we gave them that information? Do you think they would make the right decision?" This is the kind of discussion which should be part of the job design process.

DESIGNING FEEDBACK SYSTEMS INTO THE JOBS

The group's attention should next focus upon the methods through which employees will know how well they are performing. The question before the group is, "What information should the job incumbent be receiving and what is the most direct way to receive it?" In attempting to answer this question, several more specific questions must be raised, among them:

—With the work now assigned on a client basis, is it possible to provide productivity reports and quality reports to each individual for his or her group of clients?
—Can performance data be provided for each group of machines?
—Are lab reports directed back to the employee rather than to a supervisor?
—What information will they need to exercise the decisions expected of them?
—What sources of information does supervision now receive? Can this be shared with employees? Should employees receive this information direct?

These and similar issues, should be explored at this time. Typically, many of the changes made during the previous stages of the design process will have the joint effect of increasing the flow of feedback. For example, if all employees are going to be involved in solving problems for their group of clients and will receive written and/or telephone communications from them, this change has a feedback aspect to it. Or, machine operators may be permitted to make adjustments on the basis of lab reports, which are now to be channeled directly to the operators. This change also has an effect on the feedback part of the job.

Very often managers and supervisors are quite innovative in devising sources of feedback. The managers of a keypunch unit provided monthly printouts on each keypunch operator's throughput and error rates. Once a month every operator received her own printout. On it were the data on her performance, plus data for the unit as a whole.

The carding department of a textile mill asked operators to check the appropriate box on a specially designed form every time a carding machine was down. At the end of the day, the operators transferred the information to a daily record sheet. Once a week, the operator, mechanic, and supervisor would meet to discuss problem machines and to set up a repair schedule. Lab reports were also sent back to operators who discussed them with supervisors.

The key characteristics of feedback are that it be as immediate as possible, nonthreatening, and useful in helping the employee improve his performance. Experience has shown that negative feedback is not discouraging if the employee has an opportunity to improve upon his performance. The preferred flow of feedback is from the source direct to the employee, with the employee approaching the supervisor on problems.

When feedback systems have been identified for each job, the jobs should match the three-part model of an enriched job presented in Chapter 3. The total redesign process cannot be completed in only three or four days. For example, often it is necessary to study volume counts in order to determine whether equal client assignments are possible. Or contingency plans may be necessary for certain times of the year when the new job designs may prove ineffective—at year-end closings, for example.

What can be completed in the workshop is a basic outline of what the jobs should look like. This outline, while subject to modification as additional data are collected, can serve as a basis for the group to begin work on the development of plans for actually implementing the changes. Development of these plans will be discussed in Chapter 7.

FURTHER COMMENTS ON THE REDESIGN OF JOBS

The process just outlined represents a systematic approach to the redesign of jobs which maximizes the possibilities of arriving at a set of jobs which are both enriched and effective for the work unit in question. It is an alternative technology to the general brainstorming approach which emerged from early job enrichment studies. The reader will note, however, that brainstorming remains a valuable method for generating creative thinking at various stages of the design process.

Because the three parts of a job are interdependent, the group cannot focus on any one part of the design process without making modifications in all three. Throughout the redesign process, the participants should view each job as a complete system within itself.

Use of a *job control sheet* like the one illustrated in Exhibit 7 can help reinforce this perspective. The job control sheet is another way of representing the model of an enriched job. Every idea for a job design change which is agreed on should be entered on the sheet under the column or columns it affects.

Some ideas may change only one part of a job, while others change two or more. For example, allowing clerks to complete an additional form adds only a task to the job. Answering phone calls from customers potentially adds a task (answering the phone), decisions (if the clerk is to resolve customer problems), and feedback (gives the opportunity to satisfy a customer or find out about a mistake the clerk made).

Use of the job control sheet helps the group avoid some of the pitfalls of job redesign by continually providing a view of the job as a complete system. For example, if the changes simply enlarge the job by loading in more tasks without opportunities for control or feedback, the job control sheet will make this readily apparent. If certain changes in the task structure

Exhibit 7. Job control sheet.

POSITION: POLICY RATER—PERSONAL, AUTO, HOMEOWNERS, AND MARINE

Client/Situation	Functions	Tasks	Problem Control and Decision Points	Relevant Feedback
Specific set of independent agencies (reinforced by direct agent contact; agents will be notified as to which rater handles their business).	1. Process new business.	A. Review application. B. Call agency direct for any necessary additional information. C. Compute rates. D. Type policy. E. Check for correctness. F. Place in mail basket.	1. Respond to agent questions on price classifications, policy status, application status. 2. Initiate credit investigation on renewal business where it appears necessary. 3. Set daily priorities of work.	1. Phone calls direct from agents. 2. Weekly throughput figures. 3. Weekly service report. 4. Weekly error reports.
	2. Process renewal business.	A. Review application.		

also imply increased decision making, the job control sheet will make this more explicit.

For example, in handling phone calls, what are the kinds of problems the clerk is most likely to have to deal with? What authority will the clerk have to resolve the problem? The kinds of problems the clerk will have authority to deal with should be specifically spelled out. If the clerk doesn't have the authority to deal with most of the calls received, it will not be a very enriching experience. As new ideas for feedback sources are developed, should changes be made in the task and authority structure of the job to permit the employee to best utilize the information?

Those are questions which tend to be raised as the group completes the job control sheet. It is recommended that the group fill in the sheet throughout the redesign process as it agrees on changes. The job control sheet is an analytical tool; it does not automatically produce good jobs. Therefore, its effectiveness depends upon the ability of the group to use it. The job enrichment specialist should have the group be as specific as possible in completing the columns. Throughout the design process the specialist must challenge any limiting assumptions made by the group. His role is to help group members think through their implicit and often unrealized beliefs about the organization of work.

Considering the job as a whole system changes the perspective which many managers have had of the way work is organized. We have tended to be task centered, looking at fragmented tasks rather than complete jobs. Some critics of job enrichment have commented that it is impossible to add decision making into many jobs, pointing out that a keypunch operator, for example, must punch her keys in the specified order and no discretion is possible.[6]

Such an argument, made by a consulting industrial engineer of national reputation, reflects the narrowness of our traditional perspective. Admittedly, there are many jobs which are difficult, if not impossible, to enrich. However, there are many more jobs in which considerable change is possible once we recognize the importance of analyzing jobs as total systems.

Changing work flows so that employees can take a more active role in the scheduling of their work, providing more complete information on what is happening on the job, involving employees in the problem-solving process—these, too, are aspects of an individual's job, and they represent opportunities for managers to tap abilities which have been ignored by traditional methods of organizing work.

REFERENCES

1. The human resources model has been discussed in Chapter 2. A more complete discussion of the two models can be found in Raymond E. Miles, "Human Relations or Human Resources," *Harvard Business Review*, July–August 1965.

2. Robert H. Schaffer, "Management Development through Management Achievement," *Personnel*, May–June 1972.

3. Robert N. Ford, *Motivation through the Work Itself* (New York: American Management Associations, 1969).

4. Ibid. See also Merrill E. Douglass and T. Stephen Johnson, "Successful Job Enrichment: A Case Example," *Atlanta Economic Review*, November–December 1974.

5. Credit for the basic elements of this technology must go to David A. Whitsett, who began early to experiment with the methodology of redesigning jobs. Bruce Duffany, a former associate of mine now with AT&T, has also influenced my thinking in this area.

6. Mitchell Fein, "Job Enrichment: A Re-evaluation," *Sloan Management Review*, Winter 1974.

7

managing job changes

Once jobs are redesigned, the problem becomes one of converting from the structure which presently exists to the one which has just been designed. How well the conversion process itself is managed can have a significant effect on the success of the job enrichment effort.

Plans, no matter how carefully developed, will not prove effective if they are poorly implemented. How the changes are introduced to employees, the sequence in which the changes are introduced, the pace at which the changes are made, modifications in the changes as a result of feedback from employees —all of these are important factors in the conversion process.

DEVISING THE CONVERSION PLAN

In the first major formal job enrichment efforts, changes were implemented at a predetermined pace. Each change in the job structure affected all the employees in the unit at the same time. This method of implementation became known as broadsiding.[1]

One effect of the broadsiding approach to implementation

was that productivity frequently declined for a period of weeks until the changes settled in. This was because the pace of implementation, while acceptable to some workers, was too quick for others and it took time for them to adjust.

Experience has shown that the decline in productivity can be avoided if changes are introduced on a selective basis, with the jobs of the best workers being revised first and those of the other workers being changed over a period of time. Selective implementation not only allows managers to avoid temporary losses in performance but, as will be discussed later in this chapter, has taught us much about the psychology of organization change and how to manage through the structuring of work itself.

Changes in individual jobs should be done, then, on a selective basis. The first step is to analyze the capabilities of the current work force against the skill requirements of the new job. This can be accomplished with the chart, or matrix, illustrated in Exhibit 8.

Across the top of the chart are the specific skills, decisions, and feedback sources which make up the new job. Along the left side of the chart are the names of employees. Check marks indicate which employees can currently perform what tasks. At this point, the supervisor has a visual picture of his or her unit's capabilities.

The next step is to select a group of employees with whom the supervisor wants to begin the change effort. These employees should be the ones in whom supervision has the most confidence. No special number exists. Usually in a unit of 20 employees, supervisors select five or six. In a unit of ten employees, three or four may be selected. But the exact number should be left up to the supervisor.

As in the redesigning of the jobs, the principles of management development which were put forth in Chapter 6 should not be forgotten. Supervisors should be allowed to proceed at a pace they feel comfortable with. After they have experienced some success in utilizing job enrichment principles, they will become more aggressive. The job enrichment specialist should

Exhibit 8. Chart for scheduling training and job changes.

Name	Process A Accounts	Process B Accounts	Correct Total Summaries	Assign Group of Agents	Answer Agent Complaints
Robert B.	X	2-25 ✓	3-18	3-30	3-30
Alice S.	2-29 ✓	X	3-18	3-30	3-30
John R.	2-29 ✓	2-25 ✓	X	4-15	X

Legend

X — Can already do.

3-30 — Date training should be completed.

2-29 ✓ — Training completed and change implemented.

be concerned, however, that especially enthusiastic supervisors do not try to implement too much too soon. Experience has repeatedly demonstrated that broadsiding changes results in initial performance problems.

When the initial employees have been selected, supervisors should set target dates for each individual's completion of whatever training may be necessary to implement a given item. These dates are entered in the top half of the appropriate block on the chart and become an implementation schedule. When a change item has been effected for a given employee, the date should be recorded in the lower half of the block. Then anticipated implementation dates for the other employees should be filled in. Over a period of time, the chart becomes a record of whether or not the implementation of job enrichment is proceeding on the projected timetable.

When a new employee joins the work unit, his or her name should be added to the chart. The new employee should be told that while he is starting to work on only one or two tasks, a specific schedule exists for him to learn a more complete task. Setting target dates for the employee tends to overcome the problem that arises when further training is put on the back burner.

Once, a manager in the field office of a life insurance company observed that the chart resembled a form which had been sent out by the training department. He located the form which, in principle, was the same as the chart. It had never been used. Job enrichment structures a situation where managers and supervisors learn the value of a formal employee development plan.

In determining the sequence of changes, the changes which should be implemented first are those which are most basic and need to precede the others. For example, in a keypunch unit the following job changes were to be made in the following order:

1. Assign responsibility for punching a particular job to an individual.
2. Have the keypunch operators inspect the media they receive for legibility; if the media are illegible, they can send them back.
3. Make sure that jobs for a particular group or account always go to the same keypunch operator.
4. When errors are discovered, feed back the details to the operator who made the error.
5. Let some operators decide whether or not their work should be verified.
6. Arrange for departmental contacts for certain operators.
7. Let some operators schedule their own day (set down priorities).

In the example, the first change should precede the second because if a job is split between two or more operators, any decision to return the media would have to be made jointly. This would be an awkward and time-consuming process.

The first change was the first step toward implementing change three. Before making permanent job assignments, the supervisor wanted to get a better feel for the workloads which would be involved.

Implementing change three made changes four and five easier because responsibility for getting a job punched properly would be fixed. Change three had to precede changes six and seven since operators would need fixed job assignments if they were going to contact user departments to work out problems and set priorities. Otherwise different operators would constantly be contacting the various departments and no continuity of service would evolve.

Additionally, change four preceded change five because if operators were to decide whether or not their work on a particular job should be verified, they would need a good understanding of the kinds of errors they would be most likely to make.

The foregoing case illustrates the logic which should underlie decisions regarding the order in which changes are to be implemented. The usual sequence is a series of changes making the job more complete, followed by changes which increase an employee's authority over his job, followed by more completeness and feedback changes which make possible more authority changes.

Usually a period of eight weeks or so elapse after the workshop before implementation plans are sufficiently firm for supervisors to begin approaching workers about the changes. Eight weeks is an average figure; the time frame may be less or considerably more depending upon the complexity of the changes and the speed with which the group works.

Regular weekly meetings should be held to guarantee that progress continues to be made. Without the inputs of these meetings, progress may be slowed as supervision becomes involved in other activities. By scheduling weekly meetings, completing the implementation plan remains a priority item. These meetings become a vehicle through which the job enrichment specialist can help the group avoid the pitfalls discussed in Chapter 4.

APPROACHING EMPLOYEES

Throughout the job redesign process, supervisors should be low-key in their explanations to employees about what is happening; that is, they should be straightforward and specific about what they are trying to do, while avoiding the use of buzzwords, hard-sell techniques, and promises which may not be fulfilled. By "buzzwords" are meant terms like "job enrichment," "participative management," and the like. Such words carry different connotations to different people. In fact, they have been employed in so many different contexts in the popular media that they may confuse more than they clarify. Also, if the theory of structure change presented in Part One of this book is correct, the job changes should have an impact on employee behavior and attitude without a lot of fanfare about the program.

During the diagnostic study, employees should be told that the staff specialist is interviewing them at the request of managers to learn as much as possible about employee attitudes regarding their jobs. It is hoped that perhaps some things will be identified which can be changed for the better.

When the supervisors go to the workshop, employees should be told that the participants are going to a management workshop where they will talk about different ways of managing.

Upon returning from the workshop, supervisors should say they have developed a lot of ideas, which when thought through will be shared with the employees to get their opinions. All of the above statements are true and describe what is taking place in a low-key fashion.

Once implementation plans have been devised, supervisors are ready to approach their employees about the changes. Each of the employees who have been selected for the initial changes should be approached individually. The supervisor should say that he or she has been thinking quite a bit about how work is organized in the unit and feels that the following changes might be a better way. It should be explained that the supervisor wants to begin with a few people to get their reactions. The supervisor should state that he would like the employee to learn the new tasks and that the employee and supervisor will talk at least once a week to see how the changes are working out. Then the employee should be asked if he would like to try it.

Prior to approaching the employees, the supervisors should have discussed what possible reactions they may get and agree on how they will respond. For example, if the employee asks about money, the response should be, "If the changes work out and become permanent, we will have the job re-evaluated in terms of compensation. However, it is too early to tell." If the employee says no, he should not be forced to participate. The supervisor should state that if the employee doesn't want to be involved in the study, he doesn't have to be.

Selective implementation has revealed some interesting characteristics of employee responses to change. Experience has shown that when a group of employees is individually approached about job changes, roughly a third of the group agrees to participate upon having the changes presented to them. Approximately another third agree following some discussion. The remaining employees decline to participate. However, after seeing the changes take place, most of these employees and others who were not included in the initial group approach the supervisor about the changes and ask if they can participate.

It appears that many employees are less threatened by the changes if they first have an opportunity to observe them in practice. In fact, this response from employees is a good test of whether or not the changes are truly enriching.

Another lesson which has been learned through selective implementation is that positive changes in the jobs of others often provide the supervisor with leverage with "problem" employees. Sometimes a problem employee will come to the supervisor expressing interest in the job changes. Often this employee is a capable individual who is apathetic toward a fragmented, oversupervised job. The supervisor now has a basis for counseling with the employee at the employee's initiative. Minimum performance standards (attendance, quality, and the like) should be identified and the employee permitted to begin having his job changed.

Supervisors should get into the habit of regular discussions with employees about the jobs. It is especially important that they discuss the changes on a weekly basis with the employees involved. Employee reactions to the changes should be utilized to make modifications where necessary.

If job enrichment is to sustain itself, supervisors must remain flexible and be responsive to employee inputs regarding the changes which are being made. A successful job enrichment effort usually results in improved employee attitudes regarding communicating with supervision.

Achieving effective communication may require that the job enrichment specialist provide supervisors with training in job coaching skills. Being descriptive rather than evaluative, expressing understanding, using listening techniques, identifying problems, and getting subordinates involved in solutions are all trainable skills.[2] The job enrichment specialist is in a position to provide this training for the supervisors.

As the changes are made with the initial group of employees, supervisors should adjust the implementation schedule according to their experience and begin approaching other groups of employees. This process should continue until all the changes have been made.

Completely changing all the jobs in a work unit typically takes nine months to a year. However, the process is never 100 percent complete, not even when changes have been implemented so that the work unit's fundamental structure is different. Work units are not closed systems. New employees are hired and begin working their way into the jobs. Product changes require that new adjustments be made in the work structure. Over time, supervision may become aware of additional changes which can be made.

In fact, an outcome of the change effort should be the development by managers and supervisors of skill in continually managing the structural dimensions of jobs. This is the management development aspect of a job redesign effort. If supervision learns how to relate employee behavior to changing structural conditions, a permanent change in the organization will be realized.

Once the jobs are redesigned and the majority of changes are made, the attention of managers and the job enrichment specialist should be directed toward locking the changes into place. Steps now need to be taken to insure that forces within the organization do not cause the jobs to become, once again, fragmented, functionalized, and overcontrolled.

It has been repeatedly emphasized that job content is dynamic rather than static. Forces in the organization continually impact upon the jobs of individuals. In adopting a policy of maximizing human resources, a company's long-range objectives should be to create structures throughout the organization which reinforce strategies such as enriched job design, rather than operate against them.

Once the job design changes are in place, such elements of organizational life as compensation practices, systems design, management development, evaluation methods, and systems of organization controls need to be examined to determine whether they support or tend to work against maintenance of enriched job design. These elements have a major influence on whether human resource utilization through enriched job design becomes a way of managing or a one-time project in a given work unit. As such they function as support systems to the way in which jobs are structured.

The process of considering these support systems can be conceptualized as a transitional stage of a job enrichment effort, the transition being from an intensive organization change effort to a self-sustaining method of managing.

SUMMARIZING THE JOB ENRICHMENT CHANGE PROCESS

Chapters 4 through 7 have presented a process for enriching jobs in a complex organization. This process begins with the leveraging of a job enrichment effort through consideration of the role of the job enrichment specialist and selection of a key man. It continues with the determination of job enrichment feasibility and of a method for redesigning jobs, followed by the actual implementation of changes. The need for support systems, discussed briefly here, will be given further consideration in Part Three.

Job enrichment is a strategy of human resource utilization. It is a process for capitalizing upon the observations made in Part One. Job enrichment is not a panacea, nor can it by itself be the sole element of a human resource strategy. However, implemented in the proper situation, the data clearly indicate that it can pay off significantly for a company trying to manage in a period when human resources are becoming an increasingly important factor in explaining the variance in organization performance.

REFERENCES

1. Robert N. Ford, *Motivation through the Work Itself* (New York: American Management Associations, 1969).
2. John D. Drake, *Counseling Techniques for the Non-personnel Executive* (New York: Professional Education Materials, Drake-Beam & Associates, 1974).

8

team approaches
to job design

Up to this point, our discussion has evolved around the design of individual jobs. The advantages of this approach, which has been greatly influenced by classical job enrichment, are:

1. It fixes individual responsibility.
2. It allows the employee to clearly recognize what his or her individual contribution is expected to be.
3. It can generally be implemented on a selective basis, allowing supervisors to manage the work.
4. It allows "customers" of the job in question to identify who is serving them.
5. It can be implemented in a company with a traditional hierarchical form of organization.

Some specialists attempting to deal with structurally based employee performance problems have opted for a different approach to the design of jobs: the development of a team of workers charged with carrying out the many tasks necessary for a given work unit to meet its production objectives. This approach, often referred to as "semi-autonomous work groups," is something of a marriage between job enrichment and the socio-technical systems approach to job design.

SOCIO-TECHNICAL SYSTEMS THEORY

Socio-technical systems theory, which has its roots in post–World War II studies conducted at London's Tavistock Institute of Human Relations, emphasizes the effects which technology has on social relations between workers.[1]

As a result of early studies, this school of management thought noted that some technical systems are capable of being operated by more than one order of social arrangements. Further, social arrangements have a profound effect upon the stresses and problems experienced by workers as they attempt to operate the technical system.

The socio-technical school has argued that work design theories which pay little or no attention to the effects of technology on the social relationships between workers are incomplete because they are ignoring half of the total work system; the social half.

Job design specialists influenced by socio-technical theory have tried to design jobs which maximize opportunities for social interaction and the development of group identification between individual members of a work unit. In emphasizing this aspect of the workplace, these specialists rely on research evidence which demonstrates that cohesive work groups tend to outperform noncohesive work groups.[2] Since few technologies can be operated by a single person working in isolation, the problem, as seen by these specialists, is designing jobs so that group cohesiveness is maximized.

Also, human needs for social acceptance, or belongingness, are seen as strong enough to overcome the lack of interest a specific routine task may hold for a worker. Fred Emery, for example, has suggested that although an immediate task may be unrewarding, compensatory satisfaction may be found in aspects of a worker's role which provide for useful relationships with co-workers and supervisors.[3]

TEAM PRODUCTION GROUPS

Recent work in the development of team production strategies has built on socio-technical theory by maintaining the emphasis on social relationships and placing equal emphasis on many of the concepts of job enrichment. In particular, the need for challenging job assignments, increased responsibility for the functioning of the work unit, and increased opportunity for learning higher-order tasks have been emphasized.[4] In effect, the direction is toward development of an enriched group job.[5]

The basic approach is to give a group of workers collective responsibility for a segment of the production process. Group size varies from application to application. Most of the experiments reported in the literature range from five to 15 workers. These are the basic criteria in limiting the size of the work group: The group needs to be (1) large enough to perform a set of tasks found in the production unit, and (2) small enough to allow for face-to-face meetings for group decision making and coordination.[6]

In other words, the group must be large enough to cover a basic production area, but not so large as to inhibit cohesiveness and prevent group decision making. Under its collective responsibility for operating the production unit, the group decides which individuals are to perform which tasks; copes with any problems which arise in the production process; temporarily reassigns tasks to cover for absenteeism, unanticipated problems in the work, or changing priorities; and selects members to serve on any plant committees which may be devised to deal with problems. These design characteristics are in the socio-technical tradition.

Recognizing that opportunities for individual growth and achievement are important to motivation, recent team or group production design efforts have incorporated design criteria which are similar to job enrichment. As cited above, these include attempting to provide challenging individual job assignments, increased responsibility for the functioning of the work unit, and increased opportunity for learning higher order tasks.

1. *Providing challenging job assignments.* Many of the tasks which must be performed by members of the group are, by themselves, rather routine and boring. Therefore, unless a group member elects to concentrate on a routine task, the importance of giving members additional, more mentally demanding tasks is emphasized.

Often, this is accomplished through task interchanging, or job rotation, within the group. Tasks of a menial nature are divided evenly among group members, avoiding the need to assign such tasks to one individual. In addition, opportunities for more challenging jobs are increased by item 2, which follows.

2. *Increased responsibility for the functioning of the work unit.* Typically, this is accomplished through what Richard Walton refers to as "integrated support functions." [7] Wherever possible, activities traditionally performed by staff specialists are built into the group's responsibilities. Minor maintenance, quality control, lab work, industrial engineering, and personnel activities are performed by group members.

For example, specific maintenance activities which are both frequent and noncomplex in nature can be assigned to the group. Further, the group is given responsibility for initiating major maintenance activities based on their assessment of the problem.

Under quality control, members of the group take their own work samples and perform whatever tests are necessary. Any adjustments which need to be made are initiated by the group. Some plants have experimented with allowing group members to screen job applicants when a member of the group leaves for whatever reason. Thus, the group is also performing a personnel function. [8]

3. *Increased opportunity for learning higher-order tasks.* Basically, this involves providing opportunity for group members to learn and perform all the tasks under the group's responsibility. This is reinforced by the job classification and compensation system. It is becoming clear that under group production designs, individual pay increases need to be related

to the proportion of jobs under team control a given employee is capable of performing. Ideally, there should be no limit on the number of employees who qualify for higher pay categories. The role of the pay system in supporting enriched job design will be explored in detail in Chapter 9.

GROUP DESIGN COMPARED
WITH CLASSICAL JOB ENRICHMENT

Successful team approaches to the design of work have received widespread publicity in recent years. The General Foods pet food plant in Topeka, Kansas, has been one of the most widely reported. In this instance, the team approach was installed in a new plant situation.

Among the reported savings: An estimated 40 fewer employees required to man the plant than would have been needed had standard design principles been employed; 33 percent less fixed overhead than in a traditional plant; annual savings of $600,000 in variable manufacturing costs (such as quality rejects and absenteeism); an excellent turnover and safety record.[9] The innovative structure of the plant is credited with a significant portion of these savings.

Other companies which have experimented successfully with team approaches in plant locations are Procter & Gamble, Corning Glass, and Donnelly Mirrors. Volvo's experiment with a new car-assembly plant in Sweden has produced a great deal of controversy among labor and auto industry officials in this country. In place of the traditional assembly line, teams of workers assemble the various sections of the car. Team members decide how work should be divided and distributed.

So, proponents of the team, or group, approach have a range of successful experiments to which they can point in arguing for its viability. Reliable, controlled observations contrasting the relative merits of team production and job enrichment cannot be made.

The most convincing data regarding the viability of either approach comes from the application of the principles in actual production situations. Unfortunately, these "live" applications are uncontrollable in the scientific sense. It is simply not possible to attribute precisely each result area to specific aspects of the changes. Further, one cannot implement both approaches in the same situation and compare results. However, given these constraints, some observations can be made.

First, both approaches seem to work for the same basic reason: The structure of the job is such that it is possible for employees to perform their tasks in a responsible manner. The expectations communicated by the manner in which work is organized are ones of trust. Workers are able to perform their jobs, learn the end results, and contribute to improving results.

Second, the team approach is slightly more flexible, being applicable to work situations in which individual job completeness (the first part of an enriched job) cannot easily be obtained. However, in general, both approaches appear to be applicable or nonapplicable under the same kinds of work technologies: Those technologies which produce complex products (such as automobile assembly plants) have proven difficult for both approaches to alter in a cost effective manner.

Such jobs, however, are a small portion of the total jobs in the U.S. economy. Both the job enrichment and team approaches have proven applicable in work technologies which are labor-intensive, such as warehousing, maintenance, administrative, and machine operator positions.

Third, in the team approach, group dynamics can cause problems as well as overcome them. For example, it takes time for group cohesiveness to develop. Anxiety and conflict between members can emerge until the group evolves a structure of its own based upon shared expectations regarding its responsibilities and how they are going to be met. This process can result in reduced effectiveness of the production unit until cohesiveness is achieved.

Even after cohesiveness is achieved, particular individuals within the group may experience excessive pressure to conform to group expectations with which they do not agree; cliques within the group can cause some group members to feel they are odd man out. While such problems have occurred in some of the team production experiments, they have not proven to be insurmountable.

Fourth, both team production and job enrichment require the development of new skills among first-line supervision. In team production, the traditional foreman or supervisor is replaced by a team leader. This team leader differs from a supervisor in that he or she is expected to perform the same functions as everyone else and is expected to be a catalyst in helping the group make decisions rather than making such decisions as a boss. For example, task assignments are to be made by consensus rather than being assigned by the team leader.

However, the team leader faces certain contradictions in carrying out this role. By way of illustration, team leaders usually have considerable input regarding administration of the compensation system. The role they play in the setting of individual pay levels places them in a position of visibly having influence over the lives of other team members. Differential pay rates are a potentially divisive factor within the group. If team leaders are to be successful in filling their difficult roles, it is important they acquire good group process skills which they can utilize to facilitate cohesiveness within the team.

Similarly, job enrichment requires supervisors to develop astute job coaching skills. They need to learn to react to performance problems on an individual basis, rather than tightening unit procedures. Supervisors need to provide developing employees with feedback which is useful rather than punishing. Skills in this area frequently prove to be quite different from those with which experienced supervisors have managed in the past. And they can prove difficult to learn.[10] Generally speaking, however, they are easier to obtain than the group process skills required of a team leader.

In summary, both approaches represent structural approaches to employee performance problems. Team production has the advantage of being somewhat more flexible. However, interpersonal tensions can prove to be a problem, although not an insurmountable one. The skills of the team leader in facilitating group cohesiveness are crucial to the success of the team approach. These skills can prove to be quite difficult to acquire.

SELECTING BETWEEN THE TWO APPROACHES

At this time, then, no theory exists which allows for selection of one of the two approaches in given situations. My own bias is toward individual job design for the reasons listed at the beginning of this chapter and in Part One. However, at times, elements of the team approach have proven useful. In particular, the following come to mind:

1. *When the nature of jobs seems to work against construction of a complete piece of work.* An example of such a job situation is the work of bank tellers. Client identification in the sense described in previous chapters, where each employee serves a specific group of customers, is unrealistic in the tellers' situation.

However, opportunities for creating teams which work together to solve service problems, set their own break periods, decide who will work unpopular assignments (isolated windows, for example), with the head teller filling the team leader role, are certainly present. Fully implemented, the team approach would represent a significantly restructured work situation for tellers.

2. *When pre-existing co-worker relationships on the job are an important part of the existing employee culture in the plant.* In such situations, if the development of individually complete jobs through task enlargement and reassignment of work threatened to break up existing group cohesion, serious problems might be created. In such situations, it would be better to utilize this cohesiveness to solve performance problems through a group effort. Thus, movement toward work groups would be more advisable in this situation.

3. *If technical requirements to perform many of the tasks of a work unit involve considerable skill specialization, so that making jobs more functionally complete is impossible, a compromise team solution is perhaps possible.*

Usually, skill specialization will hinder development of a pure work group with interchangeable assignments. However teams of specialists are possible with the work assignment such that the team covers a set assignment, meets to resolve production problems, has considerable autonomy in carrying out its responsibilities (to shut down machines for overhaul, requisition materials, and the like), performs parts of the quality control function, receives direct feedback, and so forth.

4. *When management has a strong commitment to a team approach.* It is best to allow management to develop a work group strategy to which it is committed. Management must, however, understand the full implications of the team approach, including possible problems in achieving group cohesiveness.

Also, the team approach represents a significant change from expectations about work unit structure found in most organizations. Others who come in contact with work groups, including management, must understand the difference between the responsibilities of a team leader and those of a traditional supervisor. They must be prepared to deal with other team members on a responsible basis.

Situations 1 through 4 do not represent a theory of selection between the two strategies, but rather a set of circumstances under which work groups are more appropriate than traditional job enrichment. At the moment, the two approaches are best viewed as parallel strategies for solving structurally based employee performance problems. They are distinct enough from each other in emphasis and in the kind of structure they evolve to justify considering them separate strategies. Their objectives, however, are shared; reducing structural causes of alienation and poor performance at work.

Over time, the two approaches have influenced each other

as organizations have pursued different strategies in trying to solve their problems. This mutual influence can be expected to continue. For managers, the two approaches are evidence of the range of potential options to the way we have traditionally structured and managed our corporations.

REFERENCES

1. For further readings on the socio-technical approach, see A. K. Rice, *Productivity and Social Organization: The Ahmedabad Experiment* (London: Tavistock Institute of Human Relations, 1958); F. E. Emery and E. L. Trist, "Socio-Technical Systems," *Management Sciences, Models and Techniques*, vol. 2 (1960), pp. 83–97; E. L. Trist et al., *Organizational Choice* (London: Oxford University Press, 1965); and J. Woodward, *Industrial Organization: Theory and Practice* (London: Oxford University Press, 1965).

2. Michael Argyle, *The Social Psychology of Work* (Middlesex, England: Penguin Books, 1972), Chapter 6.

3. Fred E. Emery, *Characteristics of Socio-Technical Systems*, Document 527 (London: Tavistock Institute of Human Relations, 1959).

4. Richard E. Walton, "How to Counter Alienation in the Plant," *Harvard Business Review*, November–December 1972.

5. Frederick Herzberg, "The Wise Old Turk," *Harvard Business Review*, September–October 1974.

6. Walton, "How to Counter Alienation in the Plant."

7. Ibid.

8. Ibid.

9. Ibid.

10. Some of the skills necessary for managing successfully in an enriched job situation can be found in John D. Drake, *Counseling Techniques for the Non-personnel Executive* (New York: Professional Education Materials, Drake-Beam & Associates, 1974).

part three

support
systems

Although the design of jobs is seen as central to any human resource utilization strategy, alone it is insufficient. Increasingly, it is becoming evident that structural changes directed toward improving the utilization of a company's human resources must be approached from a global, or total system, perspective. Piecemeal reform, such as enriching jobs or developing team production work groups, is likely to prove ineffective if other aspects of life within the organization are inconsistent with the work reform.

This has been made clear by actual reform efforts. Once the jobs have been redesigned (as discussed in Part Two) so that they conform to the three-part model of an enriched job, the question becomes, For how long will the enriched jobs maintain themselves? If such changes are to endure, broader changes must be made in the organization. Other elements must be structured so that they act as support systems which reinforce fuller utilization of people.

Job content is dynamic. It is affected every time a product change, equipment change, or supervisory change occurs. Because of these dynamic forces, the importance of support systems to the ultimate success of a job enrichment effort has become clear.

Support systems can be defined as those elements in the organization which can be instrumental in assisting in the survival of enriched job design. Among such elements are compensation practices, data processing systems, organizational control practices, and management development practices, each of which is an important aspect of a corporate strategy for human resource utilization. Part Three explores these four essential support systems and suggests ways in which they can reinforce the job design changes discussed in Part Two.

9

compensation and employee utilization

Compensation is a crucial support system. In the surge of literature concerning job enrichment and similar strategies, little has been written regarding the pay implications of these approaches to the design of jobs.[1] This has been partly due to the behaviorist approach of many writers and their desire to raise to the fore other issues.

However, money is, and will remain, a central factor in an employee's approach to the employment marketplace. People work to earn a living. And, in our society, the life-style enjoyed by an individual is greatly dependent upon how well he is compensated for his work. Further, research has demonstrated that pay, and the form in which it is administered, are a powerful influence on behavior on the job.[2]

Pay, then, emerges as an important element in any structural approach toward improving employee effectiveness. How an organization structures its pay system tends to reinforce certain on-the-job behavior and communicates much to employees regarding management's orientation toward them.

145

IS PAY A STUMBLING BLOCK
TO REDESIGNING WORK?

One valid generalization which can be made about the relationship between pay and the enriching of jobs is that workers do not immediately ask for more money as their jobs are made more complete and they are asked to accept more responsibility. This is true as long as (1) the changes do not amount to only job enlargement, with the end result being a simple speedup or more routine work for the workers, and (2) the changes are made gradually and selectively, with supervision being free to make adjustments based on feedback from the workers who are involved.

Experience has established that the most typical response is one of interest in learning the new responsibilities, coupled with a feeling of "At last they're recognizing what I'm capable of doing." Of course, individual workers will sometimes raise the question of whether more money will be involved. Usually, they are satisfied with a straightforward answer from a supervisor to the effect that "If the job changes work out, the jobs will be reassessed to determine whether a compensation change is appropriate, but at the moment no plans to alter pay levels have been made."

Groups of workers have just *not* refused to accept the structural changes without an up-front guarantee of a pay increase. They are more concerned about the job changes and the opportunity for more interesting work. It is important to note that this conclusion comes from actual situations where supervisors have approached workers on implementing changes in their jobs. Thus, it is based on how workers behave in this situation, not how they report they might behave in response to a hypothetical question. Based on worker behavior in actual job enrichment applications, pay has not been a hindrance to worker acceptance of changes in their jobs.

One exception to this generalization was experienced by a large insurance company whose clerical jobs were on a bonus wage incentive system. In order to undergo the cross-training necessary to make the changes in their jobs, the clerks would have lost a significant portion of time in the incentive situation. In some instances, this could have meant a loss of up to a third of what they were earning.

Although a sizable minority of the clerks was willing to take the training if it were spread out to minimize the impact on their earnings, most clearly indicated that while interested in the program, they would not lose their bonus in order to participate. Alternative arrangements had to be made to allow the training to occur without such loss.

Later, the incentive system proved incompatible with the job changes, causing the company to abort their experiment with job enrichment. More will be said on this issue later. For the moment however, this experience provides a useful addition to our previous generalization. While workers do not demand a pay increase before accepting job changes, they will not accept a pay decrease either. If conditions exist, such as a bonus plan, which may result in employees' losing money while learning their new responsibilities, other arrangements to prevent this loss should be made prior to beginning the job enrichment effort.

PAY AND JOB ENRICHMENT

That pay does not present an initial hurdle to enriching jobs does not mean the issue is unimportant. In fact, pay can directly affect the success of a job enrichment effort in two ways.

First, once the jobs have been enriched, if significant changes in responsibility have occurred over time, compensation will become an issue with workers who see themselves making a more significant contribution to the organization. This should be expected. Our society places considerable emphasis on the ideal that compensation should be related to the level of one's contribution to the enterprise.

Second, the manner in which compensation is administered places pressure on managers and supervisors relative to the development of their employees. A pay system which requires a manager to keep the bulk of his unit at the lower compensation categories, or which otherwise minimizes his ability to reward self-development, creates an atmosphere which does not encourage him to continue to emphasize job enrichment with employees who enter his unit. In fact, such a pay system provides a reinforcement against maintaining enriched job design.

Both of these problems require that pay, and how it is administered, be given specific consideration in conjunction with a job enrichment effort.

In anticipation of the first problem, after enriching jobs, the company should, at minimum, have the jobs re-evaluated using its current method of determining job classifications. Should the evaluation determine a higher classification would be appropriate, the job should be upgraded. This process should be initiated by the company as soon as the changes have been completed and managers are satisfied with the results.

However, the re-evaluation process does not always result in an upgrading of the jobs. If the classification process is legitimate, it is usually clear to the employees that the changes have not been of a magnitude to warrant upgrading.

However, should the evaluation reveal that upgrading is appropriate, it is important that the company initiate the review rather than waiting for employee discontent to surface. This communicates in very visible terms that the company is indeed interested in the well-being of its human resources. And it reinforces an atmosphere that indicates the company wants and will reward employees who are willing to become more involved in their work.

In those instances where job enrichment has resulted in the upgrading of job classifications, the additional salary costs have been more than justified by cost reductions elsewhere. For example, operators may now be performing minor maintenance, freeing skilled maintenance people for higher order tasks; or task combination may have reduced the need for checkers or quality assurance people; or down time may have been significantly reduced. Under these conditions, it is only sound human resource management to reinforce the structural changes which permitted these savings through higher pay classifications.

The second issue involves the manner in which the pay system influences managers' thinking toward the development of their employees. No manager deals with a closed system. Employees leave the organization because of retirement, death, marriage, transfer to another unit, or another job elsewhere. And new employees replace them. Or growth itself results in the acquisition of new staff.

Consequently, at any one point in time, supervisors are faced with the task of developing employees so that they are capable of performing enriched jobs. A compensation system which emphasizes maintaining a specific distribution of pay classifications within a work unit tends to influence a supervisor against emphasizing rapid employee development. This is particularly true if the required distribution of pay classifications places the majority of employees at the lower compensation levels.

Under such conditions, a supervisor attempting to maintain enriched job design will be creating a situation which eventually will place him in conflict with his employees over proper compensation for their efforts. Further, the implicit message is that, while it wants effective human resource utilization, the organization does not place enough value on it to pay for it. Under such constraints it is unrealistic to expect enriched job design to sustain itself over time.

One solution to this problem is, during the job classification review following the enrichment effort, to set a pay rate for a completely enriched job which provides just compensation for the individuals performing that job, with the assumption that it is possible that the entire staff of the unit may be performing at that level.

In reality, because work units are open systems with regard to staffing, it will almost never be true that everyone will be qualified to perform completely enriched jobs. However, the possibility that they might must be an acceptable one. Then, working down, intermediate job classifications can be set based on progressive levels of development. The supervisor's experience with setting schedules for implementing enrichment changes can provide the guidelines for these classifications.

Two basic characteristics of such a compensation approach which tend to reinforce enriched jobs are: (1) There are no longer any limits set on the number of employees which can qualify for the top rate, and (2) compensation is directly tied to a new employee's movement through a schedule of job changes for implementing job enrichment.

One large life insurance company has accepted such a compensation procedure for those departments with a formal commitment to job enrichment. Given minimum time-in-grade requirements (which are significantly less than the time-in-grade requirements under the traditional compensation structure), employees can request an opportunity to demonstrate they are capable of performing a more enriched job. The supervisor then monitors their performance for a specific span of time. If the employee's performance exceeds published standards, the next higher classification is awarded.

Although it has yet to happen, all the employees of a given work unit could qualify for the top pay classification. The company opted for this approach to specifically encourage departments to formally design enriched jobs. In actuality, the compensation practices have not changed as radically in cost as they have in emphasis. The emphasis now is clearly on effective development of the company's human resources.

COMPENSATING SEMI-AUTONOMOUS WORK GROUPS

A few companies are experimenting with methods of compensation which represent an even more radical departure from accepted practices. These plans have compensation tied to the skills employees possess, regardless of whether they are required to apply these skills constantly on the job. This represents a significant break from traditional pay systems which emphasize the skills workers use most of the time, rather than the range of skills they potentially could apply when necessary.

Innovations along these lines have come from companies implementing the team production concept. In developing team production units, it is necessary to avoid job classification hierarchies and the differences in status and rank which are typically associated with such hierarchies. Indeed, it is the desire to avoid the dysfunctional aspects of such structures which has motivated the companies to adopt the work group approach.

However, a work group, like any other production unit, is an open system, with employees entering and leaving it and exhibiting differential rates of development. For that reason, some members of the work group can perform more of the total tasks for which the group is responsible than others. Usually, these members of the group can perform not only a broader range of the skills, but also the more complex tasks required of the group.

Employees who are capable of performing either a wider range of tasks or the more difficult ones provide the group with essential flexibility and should be compensated accordingly. Unfortunately, most pay classification systems reflect the traditional "one man, one set of tasks" structure, which the group production approach is attempting to overcome.

Richard Walton has described how one company overcame this problem.[3] This plant operates with four basic pay rates. When employees are first hired into the plant, they start at an entry rate. Once they are proficient at their first job assignment, they receive the second job rate. They receive the third, or team, rate when they can perform all the jobs for which the team is responsible. The fourth, or plant, rate is awarded when the employees demonstrate the capability of performing the jobs in other areas of the plant.

In addition to the four basic rates, employees can qualify for a special skills bonus should they possess particular skills required by the plant which are not part of a regular team assignment, such as those of an electrician.

Under such a system, employees are clearly being compensated for their learning ability and performance. They may be called on to use their skills at any time, but rarely do they utilize all of them within a short period of time. Thus, the company is paying a premium in the aggregate payroll because not everyone is utilizing all of their skills most of the time.[4]

Such pay plans are not without people problems, however. Awarding different rates of pay still has evaluative aspects, and among people who work closely together, compensation can give rise to strong emotions. Walton, for example, notes that team members often question whether (1) measurements of job proficiency are appropriate, (2) everyone has equal chance to learn additional skills to qualify for higher levels, and (3) factors other than job skills are given consideration in the awarding of higher pay rates.

As with the compensation system discussed in the previous section, it appears that compensation approaches like this one need to be characterized by (1) clear criteria for movement to the next rate which are known by the workers and accepted by them as fair and appropriate, (2) equal opportunity to qualify for higher rates, and (3) a minimum of restrictions on the number of individuals who can qualify for the higher rates.

Pay is a strong shaper of attitudes and behavior at work. Because of this basic fact, it is unrealistic to expect any pay plan to avoid eliciting emotions from workers. However, it is because pay is such a strong influence on behavior in the workplace that it is important that management, in trying to restructure for fuller employee utilization, give full consideration to whether the organization's compensation practices are supportive of their efforts.

Experience indicates that redesign of jobs cannot take place in a vacuum, and compensation is one of the important support systems which must be made consistent with the new jobs. Further, compensation systems more consistent with job re-

design can be successfully administered if a company is willing
to be open with its employees regarding compensation practices.

ARE SUCH COMPENSATION PRACTICES
COST-EFFECTIVE?

From the experiences of the companies which have tried these
approaches, the answer is yes. Companies which re-evaluate
pay grade classifications following a job enrichment effort up-
grade the classifications only if the job content merits it. And
the experience has been that those companies who find the
jobs changed to the extent that significant upgrading is in
order have also recognized significant savings as a result of the
restructuring. Typically, these are situations where significant
economies of organization have been possible. (See Chapter 3.)

One manufacturer, for example, reports an annual savings
of over $100,000 per plant as a result of job enrichment after
increased expenses for upgraded job classifications are sub-
tracted. The life insurance company discussed earlier has found
its revised approach to compensation to be less costly than the
former system given improvement in performance in enriched
work units, and Walton reports a fixed overhead rate of 33 percent less in the plant with work groups compared with the old
plant.

It must be remembered that these pay practices are in
support of changes in the traditional manner jobs have been
designed. There can be no doubt that some of the organizations would be paying a premium should their specific compensation package be evaluated against traditional wage and
salary treatment of employees, which emphasizes the skills
which are utilized constantly on the job. The companies are
willing to pay this premium because such a compensation
structure allows them to continue to experience the considerable benefits of fuller human resource utilization on the job.

For example, plants with team approaches to production,
with pay based on skills rather than task, report increased

willingness of employees to help out where they are most needed. When an organization ties compensation specifically to a task or set of tasks, it gains the benefit of insuring, on paper at least, that it is "getting what is being paid for." It also creates an atmosphere in which workers say in an emergency, "That's not my job." The game works both ways.

INCENTIVES AND JOB ENRICHMENT

The merits of incentive systems as motivators capable of improving productivity have probably received as much attention in the management literature as any other topic. Pros and cons are regularly the topic of debate between managers in organizations employing such plans.

Research indicates that installing an incentive program can lead to significant gains in productivity.[5] However, the data also indicate that incentive programs seldom fully realize employees' potential productivity.[6] A major reason for this appears to be the employees' fear that the company will cut the rate should they overproduce. Group norms aimed at restricting production appear to evolve, and considerable pressure is placed on the individual employee who threatens to exceed his peers' production.

Additionally, incentives tend to reinforce very specific behaviors on the job. As a result, they appear to work best on very fragmented jobs where the worker is expected to perform an exact task. Where the job involves a variety of elements, some of which can only be measured subjectively, it becomes difficult to reflect all aspects of the job proportionally in the incentive. The result is that employees place most emphasis on those elements of the job which are most directly reflected in the incentive.

For example, a classic dilemma faced by incentive systems in clerical work situations is the difficulty of rewarding both production (number of pieces handled) and quality (scarcity of errors). Some clerical incentive systems have tried to reflect both productivity and quality by basing compensation on the number of pieces completed, but deducting payment for those pieces which must be done over because of mistakes. Many times the clerk must redo the piece and cannot count the time spent correcting mistakes on the time card. The problem is that it is still basically production which is being rewarded. Poor quality is penalized, but high quality is not rewarded. Thus, clerks frequently come to the conclusion it is best to push through as many as possible and hope not too many come back.

Under such conditions, it is not atypical for employees to view the incentive system as a control system through which management makes sure it only pays for what it gets rather than an effort to allow workers to maximize their earnings. Pay can be a powerful reinforcer. And, like all reinforcers, subtle differences in emphasis can produce significantly different behaviors and attitudes.

The use of incentives as motivators also runs into problems when the worker cannot control all of the factors which affect the level of performance being achieved at any time. Under such conditions, a worker may not be capable of maximizing earnings regardless of how hard he or she works. An excellent example of this situation was observed in a manufacturing operation in which machine operators were paid on the basis of how much material passed through their machines. The operators' basic job was to spot breaks in the material and repair them. Thus, the fewer breaks in the material, the less hard the operators had to work and the more material would be run. Frequent breaks meant a hard day's work and would result in less material passing through the machines.

Of all the factors which could cause frequent breaks, only one third had to do with operator performance. The remainder were beyond the operators' control (for example, bad material, poor workmanship in the previous department in the plant, climate of the room, and so forth). Operators could spot a problem job when it came in and would stay out for a couple of days. "You'll work like hell and not make any money anyway" was a typical comment.

In addition to the foregoing problems, individual incentives which are tied to specific aspects of a job can inhibit coordination and teamwork between workers. Therefore, individual incentives are best employed in jobs which are highly fragmented and do not require much worker interaction.

It is beyond the scope of this chapter to consider in detail specific pros and cons of incentive systems.[7] Using incentives as a motivator is a complex subject. They tend to be a very specific reinforcer and thus are very tricky to administer properly.

Given the previous discussion, it would seem that incentives are not particularly compatible with job enrichment. Enriched jobs require employees to perform well in a variety of ways; further, they are required to exercise discretion on the job and coordinate their efforts with others. A compensation system which reinforces some job behaviors and excludes others is not particularly supportive of such jobs.

For example, the insurance company with the bonus wage incentive system referred to in this chapter found its incentive system worked at odds with the efforts toward job enrichment. Even after being trained, clerks found parts of their jobs conflicted at times with those functions which counted under the incentive. The clerks tended to want to perform the incentive tasks. Eventually, the company chose the incentive philosophy over the job enrichment effort.

It is premature to state that all forms of incentive systems are in conflict with enriched or team job designs. However, it appears that many incentive systems in use today are not especially compatible with such job design strategies—that is, they do not serve to support the strategies over time in an organization and can even cause failure of such efforts. At minimum, a company with widespread incentive systems should make a management decision to modify or change its approach to compensation in those areas in which it is enriching the jobs.

These modifications include compensating employees for the new jobs, suspending incentives in enriched areas, and systematically exploring the relative benefits of each approach for obtaining high employee performance and commitment to the job. It should be noted that such a process is a difficult one in many organizations. The path is laden with problems of political turf and personal reputations among staff groups. Therefore, this process itself often needs to be part of a well-conceived team-building effort between staff units.

Before leaving the topic of incentives, mention should be made that this discussion has focused on individual incentive plans and not on group or companywide ones. The relationship between these latter plans and job enrichment is less clear. Such plans tend to have less motivational impact on behavior because the relationship between pay and individual performance is less direct. They do appear to have a less restrictive effect upon the performance of a range of tasks and group cooperation, depending, of course, on the structure of the particular incentive plan.

One can expect that in the future, companies will experiment with job design changes and group incentives and our knowledge in this area will increase. Efforts at structuring more participation in the job by employees should include their participation in the benefits their increased contribution creates.

Job design and compensation are not independent pieces of organizational life, but rather are interdependent elements of the same system affecting employee behavior. Methods of compensation are a strong influence on the survival of enriched or team job designs. The method of compensating workers communicates in a very direct manner the behaviors which the organization most values. Pay systems, then, are an important consideration in any plan for human resource utilization.

REFERENCES

1. For an overview of this problem, see David Caulkins, "Job Redesign: Pay Implications," *Personnel*, May–June 1974.

2. For a complete review of the positive and negative effects of pay on performance, see Edward E. Lawler, *Pay and Organizational Effectiveness: A Psychological View* (New York: McGraw-Hill, 1971).

3. Richard Walton, "How to Counter Alienation in the Plant," *Harvard Business Review*, November–December 1972.

4. Caulkins, "Job Redesign: Pay Implications."

5. A good discussion of these studies can be found in Edward E. Lawler, *Motivation in Work Organizations* (Monterey, Calif.: Brooks/Cole, 1973), Chapter 6.

6. For example, see William F. Whyte et al., *Money and Motivation: An Analysis of Incentives in Industry* (New York: Harper & Brothers, 1955).

7. The reader interested in exploring the subject in considerable detail can get an excellent start by reading Lawler, *Pay and Organizational Effectiveness;* and Whyte, *Money and Motivation.*

10

data processing systems and good job design

Data processing systems design people are one of the most important of the organization elements which can support enriched job design and assist in its survival. Every time a new data processing system is implemented, or an existing one is refined in some manner, the content of individual jobs is affected. This is particularly true of paper processing industries such as insurance, banking, credit card companies, and other service industries with large clerical support forces. This chapter discusses the role data processing systems designers can play in both spreading and maintaining job enrichment in organizations.

IMPACT OF DATA PROCESSING SYSTEMS ON JOB STRUCTURE

For purposes of illustration, consider the job of policy rater in casualty-property insurance companies. Raters are the clerical people who compute the prices for a given insurance policy. Traditionally, the job has involved checking rate manuals for rates on an insurance policy, using the rate to compute a price for the policy, figuring any discounts or surcharges which may be involved, setting the policy up to be typed, and maintaining files on policyholders. Raters would also iron out problems or answer customer questions as to why a policy was priced as it was.

In most insurance companies, much of the rater's job has been computerized. Prices and adjustments are figured by the computer, and files are on a master record stored in the memory bank. In dealing with problem situations, underwriters or account executives obtain a policy's history from the master record. Although the job title frequently remains the same, the rater is now a coder preparing information for data input according to a routine set of program requirements.

Properly implemented, such systems can allow the company to deal effectively with increasing volume while controlling labor costs. The potential for faster customer service is surely an advantage as well. Finally, such systems often remove many of the minor irritations previously found in the rater job.

It is equally true that many of the interesting and challenging aspects of the raters' job have been destroyed. The opportunity to work with numbers, responsibility for records, and involvement in solving customer problems no longer exist. The job has become much more routine and repetitive.

Dull, uninteresting work is not an automatic outcome of computerization. Complaints by managers that system requirements prevent them from providing more interesting jobs for their employees are often simply not true. However, unless data processing systems designers become more actively involved in the way employees interface with the systems they design, unenriched jobs are a likely outcome.

In addition to being supportive to the efforts of job enrichment specialists, systems designers have a more direct interest in the nature of the jobs which result from their systems. Increasingly, systems design analysts are recognizing the influence their systems have on the human element in organizations.[1]

More specifically, there is a growing awareness that systems designed to consider the psychological needs of the people involved are less likely to experience operational difficulties due to lack of employee motivation or, worse, to resistance from informal employee organizations. Many systems fail to realize projected levels of effectiveness because of high error rates, part of which is traceable to disinterest and carelessness on the part of the clerical personnel. To the extent that enriched job design can result in reduced error rates, system effectiveness is improved.

Additionally, sometimes unanticipated problems due to multiple handling of paper result in increased costs associated with the system. Enriched job design can often deal with these kinds of problems (for example, see the discussion on economies of organization in Chapter 3).

AN EXPANDED ROLE FOR THE SYSTEMS ANALYST

Counteracting the tendency toward uninteresting work as a product of implementing data processing systems requires a concentrated corporate effort on many fronts. One element of such an effort involves rethinking the traditional role of the systems design analyst in relation to the user department. Although primarily an information specialist responding to the needs of managers, he is also affecting the jobs of the human element in the company and is in a position to raise job design issues with managers. Specific avenues of action are available to the analyst in helping to overcome the reasons why bad jobs result from systems.

Some specific ideas for action are:

1. *Providing systems and programs which are as flexible as possible with regard to opportunities for the people to experience an enriched job.* Implementing this item requires the training of systems design analysts and programmers in the characteristics of enriched job design and providing a set of basic principles which, wherever possible, they should incorporate into their programs.[2] Examples of such principles are:

—The program should make it possible for the same employee to handle a wide variety of transaction types. (Allows for task combination.)

—A single employee should be able to complete a transaction without the need to pass it on to another employee. (Allows for task combination and customer identification.)

—Computer-produced outputs should allow for the identification of the employee who made the transaction appear. Avoid blanket use of a manager's name. (Makes customer identification possible; also provides for direct feedback.)

—If at all possible, data should be entered in a conversational mode to allow for immediate feedback of validity checking and errors. (Provides for direct feedback.)

—Error outputs should be in the form of self-explanatory messages rather than codes. (Provides for direct feedback; also assists employees in correcting problems themselves.)

Systems and programs which utilize those principles as part of the logic provide for greater job enrichment possibilities. Some of them do require a slight loss in machine efficiency regarding core memory utilization and write-out time. In smaller companies where a programmer may be under pressure to use as little core K as possible, this trade-off may be a problem. For larger corporations with the latest generation hardware, it should be less of a problem.

As one systems man in a large company told me, "We have got to stop thinking totally in terms of machine efficiency and consider the total picture." Such a change in perspective is the first step toward "inclusive system design." [3]

2. *Expanding the scope of data collected when researching a system.* When designing new data processing systems, the analyst consults with the user to obtain information regarding the kinds of transactions that occur, who initiates them, who receives them, what steps are involved in completing the transaction, what records are kept, and the like. These data are used to understand the basic information flow and identify transactions to be made by the system. The analyst also obtains

information on the task structures of the job of each individual involved and relates this to the data on information flow.

The analyst should ask himself what the new system will do to the existing task structure and what opportunities for enriching the new task structure exist. These possibilities can be fed back to management under the heading "In order to maintain employee motivation, you should consider . . ." In many instances, this might be management's first introduction to the importance of job content in motivating employees.

3. *Anticipating client identification requirements.* Sometimes, systems design analysts view the client as the organization in which the system is to be implemented (casualty-property, the trust department, and so on). In reality, however, the real clients of the system are the people or organizations which depend for service upon the unit in which the system is to be installed. The analyst should attempt to identify who the direct customers are of the organization in question; those whom the unit deals with most directly (is it the client, the agents, or the insureds, or other departments, and so forth?).

In designing the system, the analyst can use this information in at least two ways. First, his program can reflect opportunities for employees to relate directly to the primary clients (for example, as previously discussed, if the agents are the primary client, all transactions to agents should provide for the employee's signature). Second, the analyst can suggest the distribution of work assignments be done on a customer basis rather than a functional basis, calling managers' attention to elements in the program which make this possible.

4. *Avoiding the superguru syndrome.* In doing feasibility studies for job enrichment, one of the structural clues for enrichability is the existence of what can be called "supergurus," [4] individuals who are highly developed technical specialists who solve problems or complex cases. From a job enrichment standpoint, supergurus create two problems: (1) Often they have the most interesting parts of everyone else's job, and instead of teaching others their skills, they do the work themselves, thereby (2) retarding the development of others.

Implementation of a new data processing system frequently results in the creation of supergurus. The user department is requested to select an individual to attend a school on the new system. Later, this person becomes the "office coordinator" for any problems which arise. All too often, this new role becomes part of his or her routine job. Other employees regularly refer problems or complex cases to the coordinator. This individual may even become protective of his expertise if he comes to view it as a plus for him with his superiors. The results? One employee in the unit comes to learn and understand the new system to the point of problem solving and obtaining a sense of responsibility for its operations, while most of the others remain largely uninformed.

When implementing new systems, the analyst should emphasize the value of making the new learning opportunities created by the system available to as many employees as want it. Training programs can be suggested, with the office coordinator's role being that of imparting knowledge, not solving problems.

The system itself can reinforce these suggestions by routing exceptional cases back to the employee who originally submitted a case, and by using a conversational mode to allow for fewer confusing codes. Development of clear, nontechnical training material is another way systems designers can help guard against creating supergurus.

5. *Identifying the discretionary aspects of the system.* In some circumstances, it is unclear how a case should be handled. A set of characteristics may combine in a way which the system is not prepared to handle. A manager must then make a decision on the case.

Some of these situations are identified by the analyst in advance. The probability of their occurrence is such he does not build them into his system. Rather, the possibility and criteria for handling these situations are included in supplementary material. Others emerge as the system is implemented and a system liaison person helps managers deal with the

problem. In either case, the considerations which go into deciding how such a case is to be processed should be part of every
employee's training and not left to one employee or manager.

6. *Providing flag service to the job enrichment specialist.*
In companies with an active job enrichment effort, the systems
designer can inform the specialist in charge of the job enrichment effort whenever a system having a high impact on existing jobs is implemented.

If the systems designer has already discussed the job enrichment possibilities with key managers of the client department, the ground will have been broken for the job enrichment
specialist to approach the managers. In those areas in which a
job enrichment specialist is already working, the specialist,
managers, and systems designer can explore the job enrichment
implications of the system from the initial stages of the design.

The extent to which any one of these activities is pursued
is a policy decision on the part of data processing management.
Potential policy orientations regarding the role of the systems
designer in creating more interesting work range considerably.
At one end of the continuum is implicit support of good job
design through developing systems which are as flexible as
possible in allowing for possible job designs and communicating this to the managers. At the other end is the decision to
acquire the appropriate skills and provide job enrichment
consultative services when implementing systems. Obviously,
a broad range of alternatives exists between these two
positions.

Pursuit of any course of action along these lines requires
expanding the definition of the appropriate role of the systems
design analyst beyond that found in most companies today.
Activities such as those discussed require more of the analyst's
time and therefore involve a broadening of the systems designer's base of technical knowledge. However, the decision to
involve systems designers in these activities has important
consequences for a company's efforts to maximize human resource utilization through providing interesting work.

RETHINKING THE SYSTEMS DESIGN ANALYST'S ROLE

How does a company begin to consider such a role redefinition for the systems analyst? The first step is for data processing management to assess its current capabilities and the demands on its resources and—in conjunction with other elements in the organization attempting to deal with the issue of providing interesting work (such as human resource specialists or personnel)—to arrive at a decision regarding the extent of its commitment in moving in this direction.

The parameters of this commitment include the extent to which the systems department is willing to invest in job design training for its analysts, the amount of expanded data collection it is willing to support, the emphasis to be placed on presenting the implications of this data to users, and the extent of working relationships with other staff people working on similar problems. Making these decisions will require data processing management to become familiar with job redesign principles and technology.

In making these decisions, data processing management should work closely with staff specialists charged with implementing job enrichment and related structural change strategies. The objective should be a policy statement which spells out the kinds of activities each group is prepared to participate in so that corporate activities will be coordinated.

Following the establishment of basic policy, senior analysts and programmers should be involved in the development of specific strategies for implementing the commitment. This is best accomplished through a workshop and a series of follow-up meetings. At the workshop, senior staff is (1) informed of management's intentions, (2) invited to discuss the perceived problems leading to the commitment to emphasize the human element in systems, (3) exposed to job redesign technology, and (4) provided with ideas for the development of specific action strategies. Such a session requires three to four days.

At the follow-up sessions, the staff refines these action strategies in preparing to implement them and, as time goes by, evaluates the effects of each approach and makes appropriate modifications. These sessions may be held bimonthly for a year or more.

As the strategies are implemented, training sessions will have to be provided for analysts and programmers. These sessions, in which senior staff should serve as trainers, can provide opportunities for junior staff to give input to the role redefinition process. Eventually, as the new role becomes institutionalized, the new skills will be incorporated into existing training courses for new analysts and programmers.

The important element of the process is implementation. From the first sessions involving data processing to the staff training sessions, the emphasis needs to be on setting specific objectives, converting these objectives into strategies, and putting the strategies into practice.

REFERENCES

Note: I would like to express appreciation to Wallace Harding of the Prudential Insurance Company of America. I have often benefited from discussing job design and systems design with him.

1. Cf. Jane H. Warren, "Inclusive Method of Systems Design," *Journal of Systems Management,* February 1973.

2. The most extensive set of systems design and programming principles for allowing enriched jobs which I am aware of has been developed by Malcolm McKinnon, vice president, Computer and Insurance Services, Prudential Insurance Company of America.

3. Warren, "Inclusive Method of Systems Design."

4. David A. Whitsett, "Where Are Your Unenriched Jobs?" *Harvard Business Review,* January–February 1975.

11

organization control practices

In Chapter 2, controls were discussed from the perspective of regulating employee behavior. This aspect of controls makes reference to a very specific part of the control process: the methods relied upon by managers to insure that employees behave in a manner consistent with stated organization objectives. It was noted that this regulating aspect was part of a more complete control process. How an organization approaches this more complete process determines to a great extent whether or not a climate favorable to enriched job design is created within an organization.

THE GENERAL MODEL OF ORGANIZATION CONTROLS

A considerable amount of attention has been given to the control process in research into management practices. It is generally agreed that planning and controlling are closely related activities.[1] Before control can take place, meaningful objectives must be set for the organization and strategies for realizing these objectives agreed upon.

Control is the process of monitoring feedback from activities, trying to implement these strategies, making decisions

168

regarding whether the organization is on target and, if not, taking *corrective action.* Control exists within the framework of objectives and plans for realizing these objectives.

Within the control process itself, it is necessary that key control variables be identified. These variables are closely monitored as indications of whether or not the organization is on course relative to its basic objectives.[2]

Deviation from preset standards on one of the key variables results in intervention on the part of management in the form of assessing why the deviation occurred, scheduling corrective action, and directing the behavior of subordinates so that the problem will be corrected. While specialists disagree in terminology and recommended approaches to control, the previous elements are found in virtually every discussion on control. Further, most large organizations engage in a similar process to a greater or lesser degree.

However, in most organizations the specific elements which participate in this process are diverse. Budget and other financial controls, work measurement and engineering standards, quality control reports, market penetration surveys, and manpower reports—all are examples of instruments measuring key control variables. Each is monitored from a different location within the corporation. The data comes together only at the senior levels of the organization.

The practices which surround the collection of such data and the manner in which they are responded to, represent a set of support systems relative to maintaining enriched job design. While the specific control instruments vary among organizations, all organizations employ some such measurement activity. It is up to the job enrichment specialist to identify the crucial instruments of control impacting on the particular jobs he is redesigning. Below, examples of some of the more typical ones are discussed.

BUDGETS AND OTHER FINANCIAL CONTROLS

Budgets represent a significant element in the control system of almost all corporations. The budget is the primary instrument for containing administrative cost through specific allocations. In this way each manager knows just how much he is permitted to spend.

In many firms, the ability to remain within budget is the principal consideration in a manager's performance appraisal. While other considerations may be given token consideration, performance ratings are, in practice, known to be highly associated with the extent to which a specific manager can stay below budget. In such an appraisal climate, managers are conditioned to react in terms of immediate short-term consequences.

Such a situation can inhibit the spread of enriched job design in an organization in at least two ways. First, managers are hesitant to change parts of their organizations if they perceive even a chance that the change process will put more expense pressure on their budget. Second, representatives from budget control may respond to any slight deviation from projections further discouraging any risk taking on the part of managers.

Budgets are a crucial part of the organization control process, and managers capable of operating within budget constraints are a necessity for efficient organizations. However, budget controls can lead managers to avoid implementing changes even if the changes are in the best interest of the organization. The job enrichment specialist must be sensitive to this problem and attempt to create conditions which can help overcome it.

A large life insurance company arranged for a form of budget credit, which was available for managers desiring to involve their departments in job enrichment efforts. Should implementation of initial job enrichment changes present a possibility of increasing budget pressure, for training of personnel, for example, the managers could submit a detailed proposal to management requesting a budget credit. Such credit would be for the specific purpose of permitting initial job restructuring and would be on a one-time basis only. Senior management implemented this procedure because it recognized the restraining impact budget restrictions can have and wanted to take effective steps to lessen this as an inhibiting factor.

In a large manufacturing firm, representatives from corporate headquarters contacted plant managers on a monthly basis for detailed information on costs and expenditures. It was necessary to provide plant managers with direct assurance from senior management that they wanted the managers to pursue job redesign in their plants and that should the changes result in temporary budget changes, senior management would support them.

In both of these instances, management remained concerned about the budget. They continued to seek information on budget expenditures. However, senior management also positioned themselves as willing to finance any short-term aberration in the yearly budget in order to support what they considered to be cost-effective organization change over the longer term.

Another form of financial controls, usually monitored through the controller's office, is check signing authority. In many clerical operations, check signing is lodged in the manager or supervisory position. Discussions should be entered into with the controller's office regarding modification of procedures so that responsible financial control exists within a framework which allows managers to structure situations that provide for increased responsibility and personal accountability among employees.

For example, a limited number of signatures may be authorized for check signing purposes, but the specific employees with such authorization are assigned it at the discretion of the unit manager. Under such an arrangement, the controller's office still has a list of authorized signatures, while a manager can utilize the responsibility as a motivator.

The point is that while maintaining controls, the organization also needs to structure sufficient flexibility for managers to be able to manage through the design of jobs. Managers must be able to demonstrate that they believe employees can act responsibly if *personal* control is to become a significant factor in the performance of the organization.

WORK MEASUREMENT AND ENGINEERING STANDARDS

As discussed in Chapter 3, production measurements and engineering standards can be built into the feedback dimension of jobs. However, for such feedback to be meaningful, the job incumbent needs to be permitted to get the first opportunity at improving subnormal performance. From an operation standpoint, this means identifying the level of deviation from production standards at which the employee is expected to take action. An additional level of deviation should be identified, the level at which management intervention can be expected.

This second standard can be expressed in terms of either a drop in standard below a specific point and/or inability of the employee to resolve a deviation from standard within a given period of time. The exact definition of this second standard may vary from employee to employee depending on experience and past performance. The more capable the employee, the more responsibility he or she should be afforded for solving problems of deviation from measurement standards. In most instances, the employee should be given a significant opportunity before managers and production experts intervene.

In the event that an employee requires assistance in correcting a performance deviation in measurement indicators, care should be taken to involve him in, rather than exclude him from, the problem-solving process. Often this means formal training of expeditors or teams of problem-solving experts in methods of utilizing employee skills in resolving problems. These individuals need to be aware of, and appreciate the importance of, job ownership in effective management of the organization.

QUALITY CONTROL

A specific example of quality control in many manufacturing organizations is the daily lab report. In order to prepare this report for managers, lab technicians take product samples on a regular schedule and run specific tests on the product. Any significant deviations over a period of time are called to the attention of senior operating managers.

As in the case of work measurement standards, lab standards can become a significant part of the feedback dimension of an employee's job. Lab reports can be fed directly back to employees, with employees responsible for correcting initial deviations from quality standards.

EXTENDING THE MANAGEMENT-BY-EXCEPTION PRINCIPLE

Management by exception, the practice of calling only significant deviations in performance to senior management's attention, is a central concept in many theories of organization control. In essence, the specialist needs to extend this principle down from senior management to middle management supervisors and employees. If properly structured, almost every job permits a range of deviation along several indices of performance. Within this tolerance range, employees should be permitted to seek solutions; beyond it, they should be involved in the problem-solving process.

The tolerance range, however, must be sufficient to allow the employee the opportunity to continue to control his job for a time even after performance has slipped below the minimal acceptable level. Supervisors, it should be remembered, should extend the range of each employee's control over his job on a relative basis, in proportion to the employee's level of competence. Therefore, the supervisor is, up to a point, expecting the employee to be capable of turning the problem around.

The specifics of the tolerance range vary significantly across industries. It may be anything from a slight deviation for a few minutes to a relatively large one over the course of a couple of weeks. However, if supervisors cannot systematically identify such standards, particularly with regard to experienced employees, then the often cited notion of supervisors' escaping the fire fighting syndrome is a concept which can never be realized. It is through the establishment of such standards that supervisors' true expectations regarding employee performance are communicated.

Responsibility for administering the various elements of the corporate control system is often widely dispersed throughout many line and staff offices in the organization. The job enrichment specialist then must identify what elements of the control system (budgets, work standards, and the like) have the greatest effect on the jobs which he is enriching. Then he needs to work with those responsible for administering each control element to create a situation where managers have the flexibility to manage through the work itself on a continuing basis.

REFERENCES

1. See, for example, Harold D. Koontz, "Management Control: A Preliminary Statement of Principles of Planning and Control," *Journal of the Academy of Management,* vol. 1 (April 1958).

2. See Peter Lorange and Michael S. Scott Morton, "A Framework for Management Control Systems," *Sloan Management Review,* vol. 16, no. 1 (fall 1974); and Giovanni B. Giglioni and Arthur G. Bedeian, "A Conspectus of Management Control Theory: 1900/1972," *Academy of Management Journal,* vol. 17, no. 2 (June 1974).

12

management development practices

The behavior of supervisors and managers is a crucial dimension in organization structure. How managers act, what tasks they themselves choose to perform, what kinds of decisions they make, how they respond to mistakes—all exert a direct influence upon the jobs of their subordinates. If enriched job design is to survive over time, the organization must find methods of convincing managers that they have a stake in providing and *maintaining* meaningful work for their employees.

Failure to do so can result in the destruction of enriched job design in at least two ways. First, if managers are not reinforced for maintaining enriched jobs, they will respond—once the formal redesign effort with the planning meetings and reports comes to an end—to other pressures which are being given priority by management without concern for job structure. Unconsciously, they will begin to take action which is not consistent with enriched job design. Product changes, equipment changes, and system changes (see Chapter 11) may be implemented with little consideration given to the structural impact upon subordinate jobs.

Second, supervisors and managers are replaced by others as they leave to accept positions elsewhere, retire, get promoted, or transfer. Steps need to be taken to insure that the replacements are aware of the importance of providing meaningful work for subordinates.

Providing interesting work is a continuous task, not a one-time effort. During the implementation of job enrichment, considerable care is given to structuring a situation which maximizes the likelihood that managers will have a positive experience in redesigning jobs (see Chapter 4). Once the formal implementation effort is completed, the problem becomes maximizing the likelihood that managers will continue to emphasize human resource utilization through enriched job design.

Four vehicles for solving this problem are: (1) instituting an annual human resource development plan, (2) providing new supervisors and managers with formal training in job design and related strategies, (3) achievement-oriented management development activities, and (4) the management appraisal system. Properly implemented, each of these activities can help structure a situation in which the forces of organizational life favor enriched job design.

ANNUAL HUMAN RESOURCE DEVELOPMENT PLAN

Once a year, supervisors can be asked to submit to their managers a review of current human resource utilization practices and plans for the following year. This review should include:

1. Comparisons of how job content has changed over the past year.

2. Identification of any procedural or technical impediments to providing fully enriched jobs.

3. Identification of newer people in the job system who are still learning complete jobs, along with projected target dates for their continued development.

4. Developmental plans for more established employees.

5. Identification of any problems which the supervisor feels are structurally based.

6. Lists of any other action the supervisor may wish to initiate.

The manager can then review the plan in depth with the supervisor. Summaries of these plans can be discussed at a meeting of the entire vertical slice which first participated in the job enrichment workshop. The job enrichment specialist and key man should also participate. One or two follow-up sessions can be held during the year, the purpose of which is for supervisors to share progress on their plans and to discuss any problems or pitfalls they have encountered.

Engaging in such a process accomplishes several things. First, it structures a situation in which supervisors continue to view job enrichment and human resource utilization as important priorities. By making explicit reviews of progress in this area, supervisors see such activities of theirs as visible and therefore rewardable in terms of evaluation by superiors. Second, the process provides opportunities for the job enrichment specialist and key man to continue to provide inputs to supervision. Third, participation in this process becomes one way for new supervisors to be trained in the systematic development of human resources. In brief, the process of reviewing the structure of jobs becomes institutionalized.

FORMAL TRAINING FOR NEW MANAGERS

As Chapter 4 argued in some detail, a training model has not proven particularly effective for initiating structural changes. Rather, a consulting model is necessary if managers and supervisors are to be expected to apply job design skills back on their jobs.

However, the traditional training model is a most useful reinforcer for maintaining enriched job design. New supervisors and managers should, as part of their development, attend a training workshop, the purpose of which is to provide them with a working knowledge of job enrichment and related management techniques and an understanding of the organization's commitment to the process. Such a training workshop can be anywhere from three to five days in length.

The content should include:

1. A review of the data which indicates that proper utilization of human resources is crucial to employee performance.

2. Study of how to enrich jobs, including case studies.

3. The opportunity for participants to diagnose their own style of managing, including its advantages and disadvantages in different situations.[1]

4. Introduction to resources available to assist them in modifying their styles, where appropriate.

5. Training in good counseling and coaching techniques.[2]

Each piece of the training workshop should involve participatory training exercises, such as role plays, case studies, and small group problems, to allow participants to experience and practice the techniques being taught.

Such training will prove more effective if, following the workshop, participants are given an assignment to complete under the guidance of their managers back on the job. For example, supervisors may be assigned the task of implementing a new project or policy change in a fashion consistent with the techniques taught in the workshop. Or they may be asked to develop action proposals and implement them so that an equipment change (perhaps a new type of computer terminal) does not dysfunctionally result in unnecessarily unenriched jobs.

Such follow-up allows the new supervisor to apply the techniques learned in the workshop, thus reinforcing them on the job. It also keeps experienced managers actively involved in maintaining enriched job design in their departments.

ACHIEVEMENT-ORIENTED MANAGEMENT DEVELOPMENT ACTIVITIES

Implementing job enrichment, as described in Chapter 7, structures a situation in which supervisors are encouraged to make changes on a selective basis and to learn from the reaction to the changes. Quite often, supervisors are nervous about making the changes. Success in the form of positive employee reaction reinforces their confidence, motivating them to make more changes. Thus, the supervisors learn something new about managing people through the experience of implementing job enrichment changes.

The process of achievement leading to managerial development can be applied in approaching activities other than job enrichment. Robert Schaffer has observed that making progress on an organizational problem can result in development of managerial capacity if the progress is the result of a structured, documented effort on the part of the managers and supervisors involved.[3]

Schaffer notes that at any given moment, any organization contains many opportunities for improvement which are capable of being translated into management development opportunities. Supervisors and managers will succeed in problem solving if their energy can be channeled toward solving those problems within the scope of their resources. Such success will usually increase their eagerness to explore innovative solutions to their problems.

Noel Tichy, Harvey Hornstein, and Jay Nisberg have advanced a process for getting managers, supervisors, and subordinates involved in diagnosing and improving their organization.[4] In that process, participants share the beliefs they hold about how organizations operate. These beliefs are merged into a theory of organization. Then the participants develop strategies for realizing specific goals, based on their shared beliefs about organizations.

How successful these strategies are in meeting goals are reality checks on their shared belief system. The process is designed to demonstrate to participants that they have the capacity to diagnose their organization and develop successful change strategies for improving performance.

Structured activities which are designed to provide managers and supervisors with successful experiences in attempting to meet specific organizational goals provide for learning through accomplishment. The management development process is integrated into regular managerial responsibilities, rather than being segmented apart from them. Such activities support enriched job design in that, through such involvement, the capacity of managers and supervisors to effect organization change is continually emphasized. Further, managers and supervisors are required to continue to be introspective regarding the impact of their behavior on the organization.

THE MANAGEMENT APPRAISAL SYSTEM

Continued involvement in job enrichment and related activities must be rewardable behavior for the manager in the appraisal system if enriched job design is to be maintained. Measuring a manager's performance in this area has always presented difficulties for those designing corporate appraisal systems. No easy solution exists to the problem of assessing how well a manager is developing his subordinates. However, a couple of observations can be made:

First, to the extent that an organization asks managers and supervisors to participate in the development of annual human resource plans, successful performance in this area becomes more observable and rewardable. For example, the development of objectives, which results from the plan, can become one standard of performance in the area of human resource development and utilization. The managers or supervisors who successfully meet these objectives should be explicitly rewarded.

Second, the organization can avoid overemphasizing one or two criteria to the exclusion of all others. For example, in one company the major component of the formal management appraisal is "meeting standards," keeping a unit performing within the standard set by the work measurement team. While the company talks about the importance of different measures of performance, experienced managers know that meeting standards is the important measure of performance against which they will be judged.

As might be expected, most of the energies of those managers are directed toward meeting that one specific measure. This includes stockpiling products to be counted when they need it, being unreasonably harsh in appraising their own employees so that skilled workers won't be advanced to other jobs, and maintaining only marginal quality in order to produce enough units to meet the day's requirements, plus a surplus for the stockpile. There is little motivation for managers to become involved in any activity other than maintaining standards.

The company should certainly continue to emphasize production standards. However, by giving almost no emphasis to any other criteria, a specific short-term objective is being overemphasized to the detriment of other organizational concerns.

If the managers who get ahead in a company are the ones who meet organization goals through, rather than at the expense of, their people, enriched job design can be maintained. However, should it become apparent that no distinction is made between the two approaches, a significant organization element, the reward structure, is working against long-term maintenance of strategies for more complete human resource utilization.

CONCLUSION

An annual human resource development plan, formal training for new supervisors, achievement-oriented management development activities, and manager appraisal practices are examples of pieces of the management development process which can reinforce enriched job design. Implemented, they do not guarantee maintenance of enriched jobs. But they are forces within the organization which are actively supportive of it. And, without such forces, maintenance of the job enrichment process over the long run is unlikely.

182 A RADICAL APPROACH TO JOB ENRICHMENT

REFERENCES

1. An example of a diagnostic instrument which can be effectively used in training situations is Jay Hall, Jerry B. Harvey, and Martha Williams, *Style of Management Inventory* (Conroe, Texas: Teleometrics International).

2. John D. Drake, *Counseling Techniques for the Non-personnel Executive* (New York: Professional Educational Materials, Drake-Beam & Associates, 1974).

3. Robert H. Schaffer, "Management Development through Management Achievement," *Personnel*, May–June 1972; R. H. Schaffer and R. A. Bobbe, *Mastering Change: Breakthrough Projects and Beyond* (New York: American Management Associations Bulletin, 1968).

4. Noel Tichy, Harvey Hornstein, and Jay Nisberg, "Developing Organization Diagnosis and Improvement Strategies," paper presented at NTL Institute, New Technology in Organization Development Conference, New Orleans, October 1974.

part four

overview

Frequently, executives comment, "I agree that we need to better utilize our human resources, but in companies our size it seems like an impossible task. We just never seem to know where to begin." Chapter 13 suggests an approach for the development of a strategy for more effective utilization of human resources through job redesign. Chapter 14 summarizes the crucial arguments which have been advanced.

13

creating a corporate approach to job design

More complete utilization of a corporation's human resources through job enrichment, autonomous work groups, or a combination of the two requires more than isolated, piecemeal approaches to the redesign of work. Rather, the organization must be approached as an integrated system in which all the elements reinforce the objective of providing more interesting work.

How does an organization begin? An organized approach for developing a strategy for more effective utilization of human resources through job redesign is suggested as follows.

ELEMENTS OF A CORPORATE APPROACH

Developing a corporate approach to job redesign can be seen as a seven-step process.

1. Management commitment.
2. Selection of job enrichment specialists.
3. Identification of initial work areas in which job enrichment may be feasible.
4. Diagnostic studies.

185

5. Initiation of job enrichment in selected areas.
6. Summary of results to top management.
7. Selection of additional locations and development of support systems.

1. Management Commitment

It goes almost without saying that the first step for any effort at initiating widespread changes in how work is structured within the organization must be gaining the commitment of senior management. While it is certainly not impossible to initiate a few pilot job redesign efforts without senior management commitment, those companies which have been successful in generating sustained efforts in this area have almost always done so with support from senior management. To be successful not only in restructuring jobs on a significant scale, but also in developing support systems consistent with those restructured jobs, quite realistically requires encouragement and resources which must be provided from the top of the organization.

Senior management commitment can, and often is, generated from a variety of sources. Most typically, management responds to symptomatic trends in certain indicators which cause it concern. An increasing turnover rate, poor service levels, or labor problems are all examples. Unfortunately, management is often looking for an immediate solution, while reversing such trends can take several years.

Under more positive conditions, management may initiate a job redesign effort in an effort to improve employee performance before the organization experiences any visible difficulties. Often, such a decision is the result of a series of staff presentations outlining the approaches available and the potential benefits to the organization.

As a group, contemporary managers are more cognizant of the needs of people than they were 15 years ago. They have acquired their management expertise in an environment in which industrial psychology has enjoyed considerable exposure in school curricula and in the business press. Plus, people problems have become an increasing source of concern to most organizations.

A good vehicle for establishing senior management commitment is for the senior personnel officer to initiate a series of discussions with his counterparts on the issues involved. These discussions can culminate with a meeting with the senior group, the content of the meeting being a proposed action outline for implementation within the organization. This proposal should spell out (1) why pursuit of a job redesign strategy makes sense for the organization, (2) what additional changes need to be considered to support job redesign, (3) what kind of time frame is required, and (4) what the expected outcomes are.

2. Selection of Job Enrichment Specialist

Given senior management commitment, the next step is the assignment of an individual, or individuals, to assume responsibility for the organization's efforts in this area. The basic role this individual is expected to play has been discussed in Chapter 4. In many companies, a team of specialists is created with perhaps one member of the team from personnel and another member from industrial engineering.

One of the responsibilities of the job enrichment specialist will be submission of a proposal to senior management suggesting the most logical positioning of a human resource development function within the organization. Such a proposal should be made on the basis of the organization's experience with job redesign and is part of step 6 below.

3. Identification of Work Areas Suitable for Enrichment

Once the job enrichment specialist has been selected, the next step is identification of initial work areas in which job redesign may be feasible. The question confronting the specialist at this point is structural in nature: What work units within the organization provide structural opportunities for changing jobs? Answering this question is best accomplished through utilizing the list of structural indicators that were discussed in Chapter 5.

At this stage in the selection process each indicator should be considered a clue because its existence does not necessarily mean that changes should or can be made in the structural arrangement. There may be a very good reason underlying the existence of an indicator. However, the items on the list are most frequently the structural arrangements changed as a result of implementing job enrichment. Each item represents conditions often associated with bad job design. As such, they represent clues which should be subjected to further investigation in a diagnostic study by the specialist.

All work units are likely to contain some of the indicators. It is those units which have a concentration of the conditions described by the indicators which structurally represent potential areas for initial job enrichment efforts. In such initial efforts, the specialist wants to select those areas with enough potential for flexibility to allow for a maximum experience with implementing the concepts. Work units with several of the indicators are most likely to provide this flexibility.

Working with organization charts, input from managers, and observations of various work units, the job enrichment specialist should identify how many clues exist in each area. In performing this census, the specialist may want to place arbitrary limitations on the units given consideration, especially in very large organizations. For example, he or she may give particular attention to work units with symptomatic problems like higher than average turnover or absenteeism rates, lower than average quality levels, or poor service reports.

Work units given initial consideration may be limited to those with a sufficient number of workers to demonstrate what can be done with work units of medium size or larger.

Additionally, the specialist may wish to limit the census to work units viewed by other members of the organization as being basic to the business—that is to say, those work units which perform tasks essential to the organization's basic products or services as opposed to remote or more generalized support functions. For example, enriching jobs in a part of the personnel department is not likely to convince plant managers that the concept is viable for plant jobs.

These three criteria (the existence of symptomatic problems, medium size or larger work units, and core operations) will result in candidates for diagnostic studies which will be strategically convincing to management. For example, units with pre-existing problems afford opportunities for significant improvement and the possibility of demonstrating the utility of job enrichment for solving performance problems. Also, medium size or larger units usually result in a more sizable impact in terms of measurable results. And application of the concept in core operations is necessary if job enrichment is to gain support from a broad range of middle managers.

As the census proceeds, various work units should be ranked on the basis of how many structural indicators each unit appears to contain. Those units which contain the most structural indicators are structurally the best candidates for diagnostic studies.

4. Diagnostic Studies

Having identified work units which appear to have potential for job enrichment, the next step is initiation of diagnostic studies. Gaining approval of the managers of the work unit in question is prerequisite to conducting a study.

When managers are approached, the study should be presented as part of an overall model for introducing job enrichment into the work unit. The job enrichment specialist should be setting expectations for a complete job enrichment effort with a go/no go decision point at the conclusion of the study. Before beginning the study, managers should be made fully aware of the implications of job enrichment. They should indicate agreement with job enrichment should the study suggest it would be feasible to do so.

The individual who will serve as key man should be a participant in these discussions. From the specialist's point of view, negotiating the diagnostic study is the beginning of an actual organization change effort. Therefore it is necessary that the key man fully understand the purpose of the study and the conclusions which are produced. (Conducting the study has been discussed in Chapter 5.)

5. Initiation of Job Enrichment in Selected Work Units

The specialist should begin implementation in those work units in which diagnostic studies indicate job enrichment is applicable. Over the course of a year, he or she should attempt to initiate three or four such efforts in order to provide the organization with several experiences in the redesign of jobs.

Experience indicates that starting a single trial, or pilot, effort is not an especially good approach for introducing job enrichment into an organization. Having a single pilot effort means investing the future of job enrichment in one experiment. Should something unforeseen cause the effort to be unsuccessful, it may be impossible to get a second attempt started elsewhere in the company. Should the first effort prove to be very successful, its results may become the standard against which other change attempts are evaluated. This situation can make managers reluctant to initiate job enrichment because they realize that unless they equal or exceed the results of the pilot, they won't receive positive recognition for their efforts. In any event, a single pilot is unlikely to provide an organization with the range of experiences necessary to develop realistic expectations for an expanded effort.

6. Summary of Results to Management

As soon as results from the initial grouping of job design efforts are available, managers from the areas involved should present the results to senior management. These presentations should include a description of what occurred, the problems encountered, and recommendations for overcoming the problems in future efforts. After the job enrichment workshop, usually at least two years will elapse before any reliable interpretation of results is feasible.

About this time, the job enrichment specialist should present to senior management his observations regarding what is necessary to institutionalize good job design within the organization. This proposal should include (1) recommendations for permanent positioning of the job enrichment specialist function (in personnel, systems and methods, or engineering, or through the creation of a human resources department), (2) an approach to spreading job enrichment within the organization, and (3) development of support activities to help maintain good job design (as discussed in Part Three). Experience indicates it will be at least three years following completion of step one before the specialist will be in a position to enter these discussions.

Even then it will not be possible for the specialist to present a plan for quickly spreading job enrichment throughout the company. Senior management must understand that considerable effort will be required to create a climate conducive to innovation elsewhere in the company. Fluctuations in the political, technical, and economic climate within the organization will continue to impact the diffusion of job redesign strategies for work restructuring throughout the organization.

7. Additional Locations and Development of Support Systems

Given successful outcomes of the initial series of job enrichment efforts, the job enrichment specialist will be ready to spread the strategy to additional work units in the organization. Involvement in job enrichment should be initiated at the request of managers in a work unit. Occasionally, a request will result from a manager's belief that the people working for him could be better utilized. Most often managers will express an interest because they are confronted with problems and sense support in the organization for exploring the extent to which job design may be causing those problems.

At this time, the job enrichment specialist should begin active development of the support systems discussed in Chapters 9 through 12. In some organizations, additional support systems may be appropriate.

For example, industrial engineering is a crucial element for jobs in many organizations. Strategies of cooperation between industrial engineering and the job enrichment specialist are imperative in such organizations. In one company, engineers are trained in job enrichment principles. This training is part of an effort to redefine the traditional role of industrial engineering to work more closely with managers regarding problems in the human side of the production process. In addition, engineers are being taught the behavioral aspects of organization change.

If, over the course of the next three to five years, the job enrichment specialist can succeed in developing relationships with various crucial support systems so that they tend to reinforce the goal of enriched job design, he will have effected significant organization change. Indeed, developing these relationships is as important as initiating additional job redesign efforts.

The sequence of the seven steps just presented is not intended as a one best way to organize a job enrichment strategy within an organization. Rather, it is intended as a point of departure, a framework of steps which can be adapted to the needs of specific corporations.

SUCCESSFUL ORGANIZATION CHANGE
THROUGH JOB ENRICHMENT

To expect a large, complex organization with many thousands of employees to be almost completely problem-free regarding utilization of its human resources is, in the final analysis, unrealistic. Organizations are dynamic social systems constantly adapting their structures in response to pressures for change from internal and external sources. A reasonable goal, however, is an organization structured so that at any given time a number of its employees feel that their skills are being well utilized and that they are making a meaningful contribution to organization objectives.

Within any organization there exist influences which can work at cross-purposes to such a goal. Introduction of new production systems with insufficient consideration given to the human side of the system, compensation packages which provide managers with minimum flexibility to reward outstanding performance and which place employees in competition with one another, management responses to problems with a blanket application of direct controls—these are but a few of the forces which can, over time, work at cross-purposes with the objectives of a job enrichment—human resource utilization effort within an organization.

To be successful, the job enrichment specialist must create influences within the organization which tend to negate these forces acting against enriched job design. Rather, forces within the organization must tend to reinforce the objectives of job enrichment.

A successful job enrichment effort cannot be measured by how many work units have participated in a one-time effort to redesign work. Success depends on how long the benefits continue within each unit and whether the organization appears to be on a qualitatively different direction than before the effort was initiated.

These can be measured in the manner in which the organization responds to various problems which require organization change. How are new plants and offices structured? Is the job enrichment specialist called upon to contribute to the planning process? When new systems are implemented, are human resource needs designed into the system? How is work structured around new product lines? Do engineers attempt to design flexible production processes which allow managers to manage the work itself to reflect the abilities of individual employees?

It is when the answer to questions such as these is yes that permanent organization change has been realized. By this standard, few corporations can claim success, despite the recent popularity of job redesign concepts in industry.

The job enrichment specialist must be capable of developing into a broadly skilled human resources consultant capable of helping the company not only redesign work, but also develop teamwork between managers, identify a range of employee needs, and solve problems in operations so that human resources are not wasted.

Considerable evidence exists in support of the argument that effective utilization of human resources has an economic payoff for a company. At the core of human resource utilization is proper design of jobs. However, to realize the true potential payouts, success must be measured not in terms of the amount of activity, but of whether or not the changes have been locked in. It is better for an organization to gradually change and ten years from now be a qualitatively different place to work in than to experience a flourish of activity which proves only to be an aberration from its previous direction.

14

epilogue

The preceding chapters have covered a wide range of topics. I have tried to make a case for the principle that how we design the structures which compose our organizations has a profound impact on the behavior of the people who work in those organizations. More specifically, the manner in which managers respond to performance problems—whether they automatically impose organization controls or first analyze what in the organization's current structure may be causing the problems—has a profound impact on how effectively the organization utilizes the potential of its human resources.

In many instances personal controls and group controls are more effective than organization controls because the former two communicate a more positive set of expectations. And people tend to meet the level of expectations communicated by management.

People respond to their internal feelings about the situations they are placed in. If management tells its employees it expects them to be responsible and then structures a work situation which demonstrates it doesn't believe they will be responsible, it tends to get apathetic, irresponsible employees.

Management must make employees responsible if it wants them to behave responsibly. Management must structure a motivating situation if it wants employees to be motivated on the job.

Work structure can be managed. In order to manage work effectively, managers must not be solely task oriented. Rather, they must come to recognize that how work is assigned, the degree of autonomy afforded each employee, the sources of feedback from which an employee can determine how well he is performing are all dimensions of the work situation. Because employees are flexible and responsive, managers must learn to structure work processes which are also flexible and responsive.

Redesigning work involves organization change. The process through which an organization attempts to initiate change determines to a considerable degree whether or not its efforts will prove successful. Providing managers with appropriate staff support, paying proper attention to diagnostic work, having the right managers involved in the restructuring process—all these are crucial elements for successful organization change.

Organizations are made up of several complex, interdependent structural systems. Change in one aspect of organizational structure, such as the design of jobs, requires change in other structures if the initial changes are to sustain themselves.

All of these topics have been discussed in some detail in previous chapters. Yet, we have only touched the surface. We are just beginning to learn about these complex relationships. We do not have, for example, any comprehensive set of principles which specify under what conditions group and personal controls are more effective than organization controls or vice versa. Nor does there exist a theory of job design which clearly points out what alternative designs are most effective under certain technological requirements. And despite all the literature on organization change, change remains a difficult, and sometimes painful, process for most organizations to endure.

Progress, however, is being made in all these areas. And

one thing is certain. Any organization which over the long run wishes to remain an effective entity needs to develop its own approach to these problems. The environment in which the organization must function is continually changing. The labor force available to it is better educated, more affluent, and, in many ways, more mobile than in the past. Human resources are increasingly becoming a constraint on an organization's ability to grow and perform. And customers are demanding better service which can be provided only by motivated employees who are permitted to perform their jobs.

So, in the long run, *survival requires innovation*. And that is what this book has been about.

index